E. B. Warman

Warman's physical Training

Or, The Care of the Body

E. B. Warman

Warman's physical Training
Or, The Care of the Body

ISBN/EAN: 9783337062972

Printed in Europe, USA, Canada, Australia, Japan

Cover: Foto ©ninafisch / pixelio.de

More available books at **www.hansebooks.com**

Vigorously Yours

E. B. Warman

WARMAN'S
PHYSICAL TRAINING

OR

THE CARE OF THE BODY.

BY

E. B. WARMAN, A. M., CHICAGO, ILL.

AUTHOR OF PRINCIPLES OF PRONUNCIATION IN WORCESTER'S DICTIONARY, PRACTICAL ORTHOËPY AND CRITIQUE, PRINCIPLES OF READING, RECITING AND IMPERSONATING.

FOURTH EDITION, REVISED AND ENLARGED.

"Obedience is better than sacrifice."

CHICAGO, NEW YORK, PHILADELPHIA
PUBLISHED BY A. G. SPALDING & BROS.
1891.

COPYRIGHT 1885, BY E. B. WARMAN.
COPYRIGHT 1889, BY E. B. WARMAN.

PUBLISHERS' NOTICE.

Prof. Warman has been eminently successful in all parts of the country in teaching his most valuable of all systems of PHYSICAL TRAINING for the SYMMETRICAL DEVELOPMENT of the body.

This manual is the result of years of experience in the school-room and upon the rostrum; hence we take pleasure in introducing it to the public as the most PRACTICAL work of the kind extant. It is especially adapted to the needs of schools, colleges, etc.

                Respectfully,
                      A. G. SPALDING & BROS.

AUTHOR'S PREFACE TO THE FOURTH EDITION.

REVISED AND ENLARGED.

Not long since, upon the literary sea, we launched a little barque. It was so small that, among the myriad of others, we knew not if notice would be taken of it, but sent it forth to meet its fate. We did not predict for it a voyage upon an unruffled sea; hence we built it of seasoned timber gathered from our ripened experience. We fashioned it

> "Staunch and strong, a goodly vessel
> That will laugh at all disaster,
> And with wave and whirlwind wrestle."

True, the little craft was not wholly original, for others had been built; but the design and the arrangement of the apartments were the result of our own handiwork, growing out of the knowledge of the great need of

PRACTICAL PHYSICAL TRAINING IN THE SCHOOLS AND COLLEGES.

We have met the demand, and from the various ports—Colleges, Seminaries, Schools, Homes, etc., the little barque has returned, having had a most successful voyage.

We are now importuned to rebuild and enlarge our former structure. We have complied with the request, having greatly improved every department; and we vouchsafe health and happiness to all who embark with us, and follow our directions.

PUBLISHER'S PREFACE.

APARTMENT No. 1 contains many timely suggestions as to

THE CARE OF THE BODY.

By living in accordance therewith not only will many years be added to one's life, but life will be added to one's years.

APARTMENT No. 2 has been arranged with a view to school-room conveniences, and *in*conveniences. We furnish therein our

SYSTEM OF EXERCISES WITHOUT APPARATUS.

These, with few exceptions, can be taken in very small space—even for classes.

APARTMENT No. 3 has also been arranged with a special view to class exercise in limited quarters. These can be given by children in school, while standing by the desk. In this apartment will be found our thorough, complete and practical

SYSTEM OF DUMB-BELL EXERCISES.

These have been especially prepared for the strengthening and developing of the entire body.

APARTMENT No. 4 presents, in the most concise manner, as the result of years of labor in this field of physical training, our

SYSTEM OF INDIAN-CLUB SWINGING.

Believing, as we do, in thoroughness, we have prescribed a system for the mastery of one club, ere the attempt is made to control two.

Without further ceremony, we launch the new barque with its rich cargo, trusting it will fully serve its mission. *Bon voyage.*

E. B. WARMAN.

Chicago, Ill., April 29th, 1889.

INDEX TO CONTENTS.

	PAGE
The Care of the Body	11
Physical Training for Schools, etc.	15
Whiskey	17
Tobacco Chewing and Smoking	18
To Secure Longevity	31
Degeneracy of Man	36
General Rules of Health	39
Fresh Air	42
Correct Breathing	43
Bathing	45
Catarrh	46
The Throat	47
The Care of the Feet	48
The Color of the Clothing	50
Magnetism	52
Sleeping at Will	55
Belt and Corset	60
Symmetrical Development	64
Exercises without Apparatus	67
The Lungs	68
The Chest	69
The Shoulders	70
The Fingers	71
The Wrists	72
The Elbows	76
The Shoulders	78
The Neck	80
The Waist	84
The Hips	87
The Knee	89
The Ankle	91

INDEX TO CONTENTS.

	PAGE
Exercises without Apparatus—Continued.	
The Calf and Thigh	93
The Thighs	94
The Fore-arm	95
The Chest	96
Physiological Charts	98
Key to Figures of Muscular System	100
Dumb-Bell Exercises—	102
Indian-Club Swinging (one club)	121
Inward, Right	124
Outward, Right	125
Outward, Left	126
Inward, Left	127
Poise and Drop, Left	128
Poise and Drop, Right	129
Outward Right—Outward Left	130
Large Wheel—Right to Left	131
Large Wheel—Left to Right	132
Small Wheel—Right to Left	133
Small Wheel—Left to Right	134
Poise, Drop and Inward, Right	135
Poise, Drop and Inward, Left	136
Drop and Inward, Right and Left	137
Small Side-Circles, Right	138
Large Side-Circles, Right	139
Large Side-Circles, Right (Reverse)	140
Small, Large, Diagonal, Large, Right	141
Small Side-Circles, Left	142
Large Side-Circles, Left	143
Large Side-Circles, Left (Reverse)	144
Small, Large, Diagonal, Large, Left	145
Chin-Knocker, Right	146
Chin-Knocker, Left	147
Lever, Right	148
Lever, Left	149
Inward and Forward, Left	150
Inward and Forward, Right	151

INDEX TO CONTENTS.

	PAGE
Indian-Club System (one club), Condensed for Calling	152
Indian-Club Swinging (two clubs)	155
Point, Left and Right	156
Small Left and Large Right	157
Small Right and Large Left	158
Alternate	159
Backward Drop	160
Forward Drop	161
Outward Left and Backward Drop Right	162
Alternating Outward	163
Alternating Inward	164
Double Small Circles	165
Left, Right, Both	166
The Windmill	167
Forward and Inward, Left Side	168
Forward and Inward, Right Side	169
Alternating	170
Right, Left, Right, Left, Front, Front	171
Small Side-Circles	172
Double Inward	173
Double Sweeps	174
Sides, Inward, Sweeps	175
Small Sides, Left and Right	176
Small Sides, Alternate Right	177
Small Sides, Reverse, Right	178
Out, In, Out, Under, Toss, Left	179
Right Horizontal	180
Left Horizontal	181
Check	182
Shoulder Brace	183
Full Arm, Reverse	184
Windmill and Alternate	185
The Finish	186
Taking the Clubs Artistically	187
Indian-Club Swings (two clubs), Condensed for Calling	188

"If any man defile the temple of God, him shall God destroy, for the temple of God is holy, which temple ye are."

PHYSICAL TRAINING;

OR,

THE CARE OF THE BODY.

BY

E. B. WARMAN, A.M.

CHICAGO, ILL.

"Holier than any temple of wood or stone, consecrated to divine right and divine purposes, is the human body."

We are aware that in a measure all that is good has been said before; all that is noble has been thought before; but is there less need of re-saying the good, or re-thinking the noble? We are also aware that volumes have been written on the subject of physical training, yet we fail to see a proportionate amount of benefit resulting therefrom. We naturally ask ourselves, Why is this?

Trusting that we may not seem presumptuous, we shall undertake to solve this problem. It arises from one of two causes; either that the various modes of exercises have not been placed before the public in a way to make them practical as well as pleasurable, or that such modes as have been given have been abused by unwisely using them, thereby causing the public to become prejudiced against anything that pertains to manly sports.

There is not an art, science or religion extant that cannot be abused; should we then condemn them all, or should we not, rather, as representatives of such a calling, do all in our power to exalt the true ideal, and thus establish our forces against the enemy of that which is high and grand and ennobling?

We wish to define our position at the very outset by answering the question—to what end should physical training be taught? Health should be the primary object. You have it? Then exercise to keep it. The end or aim of training in physical exercise should not be with a view to muscular development only.

The secondary object of physical training should be symmetrical development and graceful carriage of the body. No teacher should lay claim to proficiency, and no book to completeness that disregards this theory. We find, even among gymnasts, a great deal of abnormal development.

Did you ever ask a man to show his muscle? You did? What muscle? You did not specify any particular one, yet you asked him in the singular, indicating thereby that he has but one. Nine hundred and ninety-nine men out of every thousand will at once put up the arm and show you the biceps. Is it a criterion of strength? Not by any means, not even of the arm for all purposes. It is often an indication of weakness somewhere else, especially if over-developed. It is a test of strength in pulling or lifting. Such a development will not materially aid one in striking a powerful blow, for the triceps (which is used in striking or pushing) may have been neglected. To satisfy yourself concerning the development of these muscles, push against some solid substance with your right arm, the palm of the hand resting against the object; then feel the upper portion of your arm, back and front, with the left hand, and you will readily perceive that the forepart of the upper arm (biceps) shows no special development, while the back part (triceps) is quite solid. Reverse the exercise by pulling a heavy object toward you, or raising a heavy weight from the floor by bending your arm at the elbow, and you will at once feel (by using the left hand), that the muscle of the fore part of the upper arm (biceps) immediately rounds and fills out, while the back part (triceps) becomes nearly level.

An expert rower should be an expert boxer, and thus equalize the development and consequent strength of his arm. What! Is boxing manly? Yes, when a *man* boxes. Anything that a man does is manly; anything that a woman does is womanly. Next to God Himself there is nothing grander than a manly man and a womanly woman. There are many who regard boxing as brutal It is, when you make it so. So is rifle practice; so is saber exercise; so is anything that may be abused. Because you are an expert with the gloves, there is no more danger of you entering the prize ring, or developing a disposition to pommel everybody, than being an expert with the rifle or saber will develop a desire to go around and shoot or slice up your neighbor. Apropos to this we state the familiar quotation: "It is glorious to possess a giant's strength, but it is cowardly to use it as a giant."

Let the poor, hollow-chested, bad livered, dyspeptic grumbler against manly sports, come out of his little den, doff his coat and vest, breathe freely, purely and deeply of the fresh air that the Almighty has so freely and so plentifully given; then let him take up a pair of Indian-clubs, or hurl the ball, or pitch the quoit, or poise the rifle, or use the dumb-bells, or tug at the oar, and he will go back to that self-same den and acknowledge to the world, through the silent but powerful medium of the pen, that he was wrong in attacking the thing itself when his blows should have been leveled at its misapplication or abuse. We exclaim with Dr. Foss: "Let these things be done with the distinct recognition that we have a higher nature, and in such a manner and measure as to do no harm to what is best and noblest in this loftier realm."

We have spoken of health of body and carriage of body as distinct aims of physical training; but we must not stop there, for it is threefold in its mission; it will give us what the old Latin poet prayed for—"A sound mind in a sound body." Many of our colleges are supplied with a gymnasium, which too often proves a detriment, from the fact that so many of them are without a competent teacher, the lack of which compels the pupil to choose his own exercises, as well as the manner of taking them; consequently he will either overdo in the first few weeks and then cease altogether, or will resume only spasmodically, both of which are hurtful. Possibly he may continue daily, but in the absence of an instructor he will take only such exercies as are the most pleasurable to him, thereby developing one set of muscles at the expense of others. All these things need special care. Any exercise, to produce lasting and beneficial results, should be regular, but never violent. Many persons act upon the supposition that physical exercise must be fatiguing or exhausting, in order to be strengthening; such exercises are instead, debilitating.

PHYSICAL TRAINING FOR SCHOOLS, ETC.

We would prescribe a course of physical training that should be obligatory as a part of the curriculum of every school, college and seminary. The teacher, be it he or she—it is no longer a question of sex but of gumption—should be genius enough to enthuse the pupils so that the exercise will not be looked upon as irksome, but as a pleasure. But it may be argued that the majority of colleges do not have, nor can they afford, a first-class gymnasium. No first-class college can well afford to be without one, or at least some good form of every-day gymnastic exercise. It is also considered that the exercise is not becoming to a lady. It is, if she provides herself with a becoming costume.

The demands of the physical are in every way

equal to the demands of the mental. Exercise of any kind to be beneficial, should be general. If too much attention is given to the physical development and the mental is neglected, the brain will become correspondingly weak in its functions. The same rule applies to excessive mental development, drawing the much needed blood of the body to supply the brain. Brain work is much more exhaustive than hand work. Dr. W. W. Hall very aptly puts it thus: "The farmer can work from morning until night from one week's end to the other, and thrive upon it; the brain worker cannot profitably spend more than six hours out of the twenty-four. The most successful and voluminous literary men of our time, who maintain their vigor to a good age, do not spend more than four or five hours at their desk, having found that that was the limit of their endurance and pleasurable labor."

The body, also, needs the utmost care, as it is the sacred temple for the indwelling of the soul. Do our young men and young ladies so regard it when, as it is termed. they are "getting an education"? An education of what? Simply of the mind, while the body is so neglected that processes are going on which are sapping the very life from the foundation of that mind. How many weak, debilitated, half-alive men and women are knocking at the doors of our halls of learning and asking admittance. It were just as reasonable to adorn a tumble-down shanty with a mansard roof, as a physical wreck with an accomplished education.

Stand before any institution of learning and watch

the young men as they emerge from the building and pass down the street. You will find scores of them with whom the head seems running away with the body, not because the head is so large, but because the body is so small. If you want a fair representative of the average student who neglects physical culture, just put a large round doughnut on a hairpin.

WHISKEY.

Do the young men of our day realize the value of the human system when they put that thief in their mouth which steals away their brains? It attacks the very citadel, and when the brain is stupefied, what can they expect of the body? How well Shakespeare understood this when he put these words in the mouth of Lady Macbeth:

" His two chamberlains will I with wine and wassail so convince,
That memory, the warder of the brain, shall be a fume,
And the receipt of reason, a limbeck only!"

Yet, in the face of our attack on whiskey, we have no hesitancy in saying: "Whiskey is the best thing in the world for a man—when he is *dead!* It will *preserve* him. But it is the worst thing in the world for preserving a man when he is *living.*" So says Dr. Guthrie.

If you want to *keep* a dead man, put him in whiskey; if you want to *kill* a man, put whiskey in *him*. It was undoubtedly, a good thing for preserving the dead admiral when they put him in a rum-puncheon, but it was a bad thing for the sailors when they tapped the cask and drank the liquor, until they left the admiral, as he had never left the ship,—high and dry.

While we are speaking of those things which ruin our beautiful temples, we would like to say a word that would plead like "angels, trumpet-tongued, against the deep damnation" of the most pernicious and filthy habit of

TOBACCO CHEWING AND SMOKING.

The liquor question has been so ably handled by competent writers, and the tobacco question so little discussed, comparatively, that we prefer to devote more time and space to the latter. The results of liquor are so generally understood, and its evils so widely known, and its horrible consequences shunned by all lovers of peace and harmony; while the slaves of tobacco, with their pernicious habits, find their way in nearly every family of our land. Too little is actually known of the terrible results arising from this evil; though ignorance is no excuse for the violation of a law.

The filthy spittoon—cuspidore is too refined—should take its place by the side of the whiskey jug, *i. e.*, it should have no home in a refined or Christian family.

We like to say all the good we can of everything ; so we can truthfully say there is nothing better than tobacco—for removing insects from plants. Just take that pound which was bought to put in the mouth and put it in three pints of boiling water, and by pouring it on the plants it will destroy the insects instead of killing the man ; or, if the habitual tobacco user does not want to *waste* the tobacco, let him take a good hot water bath, and the water will be sufficiently permeated with the tobacco poison from his system to do its deadly work on the insects.

What effect has tobacco upon this system of ours, which we should study to preserve in all its beauty and strength? Allow us to mention but a few (?) of the evils: Headache over the eyes; nervous headache, with sickness of the stomach; deafness; partial blindness; running of the eyes; cancer of the lips; consumption, preceded for years by a cough; asthma; dyspepsia; palpitation of the heart; paralysis of the upper part of the body ; neuralgia, especially of the face, head and neck; swelling of the gums and rotting of the teeth; enfeeblement of the lymphatics; enlargement of the glands of the face and neck, making the chewer thick about the cheeks and lips; lethargy; morbid appetite for spirituous liquors; morbid appetite for highly flavored food; indistinct taste; indistinct smell; imperfect sense of touch; obtuseness of the moral sense; uncleanness of person; stentorian or snoring sleep; a sense of dullness and of great debility when first waking from sleep until one has had a chew or smoke; confirmed and incurable disease, and premature death.

We wish to call your attention to some quotations from a discourse delivered at Island Park assembly July 23, 1885, by the Rev. George L. Curtis, M. D., D. D. of Seymour, Indiana :

" The chemical elements of tobacco are decidedly poisonous to the human system, for which there are no known antidotes. The first element is a volatile oil or fat, obtained by distilling the smoke of tobacco. It has the odor of tobacco, and when inhaled produces the same sensations as smoke. When applied to the nose its pungency causes vomiting, taken internally it produces giddiness, nausea, and a staggering walk ; it is poison.

"The second element is a volatile alkali, called nicotine ; *it* is a deadly poison, next in rank to prussic acid. One drop is sufficient to kill a dog, if placed on his tongue. One drop, evaporated in a room holding two hundred people, is so penetrating that it will drive them out in a few moments.

"The third element is an empyreumatic oil, obtained also by heat. A drop of this poison placed on the tongue of a cat will cause horrible agony, convulsions and death, in from two to four minutes.

"These three chemical substances are all developed in burning tobacco, either in smoking a cigar or pipe. In the residuum of a pipe long used they exist in a dark-brown or tanny mass of offensive matter.

"If you take a mouthful of tobacco smoke, and expel it through a clean white handkerchief, you will see when it passes the fabric that it makes a black spot. Examine this black matter under a microscope of five hundred diameters, and you will see the crystals of nicotine, the oil globules and the acid. These enter the mouth with the smoke, and some of it is absorbed directly, and other portions of it after a time, and so they enter the circulating system.

"The manner in which tobacco is used is not in

harmony with any of the laws of our being, or our health. Chewing, and then expectorating, is contrary to the use designed in the making of our tongue, teeth, lips and palate. It was never intended that we should chew substances and expectorate them. Deglutition was designed to follow chewing, but to swallow tobacco is dangerous. Man is the only spitting animal known except the cat, and it does not spit until it is mad. Smoking, develops the chemical principles of tobacco, all of which are rank poisons and extremely dangerous. In smoking, the heat passes down too rapidly and causes changes which cannot be met by any anti-poisons. It turns the mouth, out of which ought to come blessings, into a chemical shop, where vile things are compounded.

"The physiological effects of tobacco are destructive of health and life. In *chewing* tobacco, the salivary glands are stimulated to undue activity. In health, these glands secrete an average of three pounds every twenty-four hours; when one is chewing tobacco he secretes from eleven to thirteen pounds every twenty-four hours. You can calculate how long it would take a man to spit himself away."

A man who expectorates that filthy tobacco juice must not *expect to rate* among the cultured and refined.

"In chewing tobacco the glands become enlarged; the microscope shows the substance congested, hardened and thickened, and the orifices hardened and enlarged by such constant stimulation.

"Give an expert microscopist a section of the

parotid gland, and he will tell you whether that person was a tobacco chewer or not. Chewing, brings some of the poisons into the system by the absorbing vessels of the mouth and throat. These injuriously affect both the circulating and nervous system.

"A cigar, wet, and laid on the stomach of a child, will produce sickness, for the skin absorbs the poison of the tobacco. In *smoking*, the *three poisons* alluded to are developed. In an old pipe, used three months, the residue in the bowl is a compound of all these active poisons.

"In Ohio, a little girl fell against the stove and burned her lip. The burn did not heal so rapidly as her grandmother thought desirable, so the grandmother,—a great smoker—called the little granddaughter to her, and, running her finger around in the bowl of the pipe, took the black tobacco juice and rubbed on the little girl's sore lip. In a few minutes the child was in violent convulsions, and in twelve hours died. The old pipe killed her.

"Tobacco also affects the heart. It causes paralysis and intermittence of pulse beats. A doctor in New Hampshire was consulted by the mother of a girl four years old, who was affected with a severe eruption on the face. The mother was anxious, from having heard stories of its efficacy in other cases, to make an application of tobacco. The physician, however, advised the contrary and left, to visit a sick neighbor. While prescribing for the latter, he was called back in haste to the child, whom he found senseless and motionless on the floor. The mother informed him that, being still persuaded that tobacco would be beneficial, she had, after he retired, taken some from the bowl of a pipe and rubbed it on the child's face. The child set out to walk across the room immediately after the application, but had not gone half way before she fell in the condition in which he found her. The physician worked an hour, resorting to various means for resuscitating the child, the pulse occasionally reviving and then dying away again, until finally animation was restored. For years afterward the child was subject to alarming nervous symptoms, and is now puny and feeble. Her constitution previous to the experiment was good, but the shock upon the nervous system was so severe that she never recovered, and probably never will.

"Now a word as to the effect of tobacco on the brain worker. Men cannot be as good students who use tobacco as those who abstain. In the Medical College of Indiana for 1883 and 1884, the students who wholly abstained from tobacco stood, in final examination, at 87.33, while those who smoked, or chewed and smoked, stood at 80.14. Dr. Dio Lewis made the statement that 'not a man addicted to the use of tobacco has taken the honors in Harvard College for the past fifty years, though five out of every six students use the weed.'

"Many years ago, the Council of Berne, in Switzerland, recognized the principle that 'tobacco is a deadly foe to mind development,' and they at once issued an edict prohibiting the use of tobacco to youths under fifteen years of age.

"The French Minister of Public Instruction, after classifying the pupils into smokers and non-smokers, finding the latter to be the better students, contemplated the prohibition of the use of tobacco in all the colleges of France."

We anticipate the question in reference to the harmless (?) cigarette. If you have any pride at all in regard to the body; if you wish to retain the home of the soul as a fit dwelling place thereof; if you have any ambition, any of you young men, to become athletes, listen to the words of Mr. J. M. Laflin, a New York athlete, when interviewed by a New York *Sun* reporter, touching the subject. He replied: "There is no engine of destruction known to humanity to-day doing more damage than the popular cigarette."

We have no doubt that there may be those who claim to have used tobacco, in some form or other, many years, and have not experienced any serious results. We know of a man who lived to be over one hundred years old, and had used it all his life, and that to excess. *He* lived, but he transmitted the poison to his entire family of children, all of whom died at an early age. We might say, "Poor man! we *pity* your *weakness;*" but we extend our sympathy in another direction and say, "Poor wife! we *admire* your *strength.*"

It is wonderful how much this system of ours will endure before it yields to the inevitable. Let no young man take the example, just given, as a criterion.

It should be reason enough for abandoning the use of tobacco that it produces such a foul breath and such filthy habits. Can we find nothing in the Scriptures concerning it? Yes, and he who uses the weed, especially to excess, may take consolation therefrom: "Let him that is filthy be filthy still."

The odor of the tobacco user's breath is abominable. Charles Lamb, in writing his "Farewell to Tobacco," gives us the following:

> "Stinking'st of the stinking kind,
> Filth of th' mouth and fog of th' mind;
> Africa that boasts her foyson
> Breeds no such prodigious poison."

An expert will tell by the breath the character of the materials passed down the throat or in the mouth. There is an alcohol breath, a beer breath, a wine breath, an opium breath, an onion and garlic breath, and a tobacco breath. But the breath of onions and garlic is the ambrosia of the night-blooming cereus, or the balm of a thousand flowers, or the spicy odors of Ceylon's isle, when compared with the tobacco user's breath.

There was an old colored woman with whom some one expostulated concerning her offensive breath, saying: "Mammy, your breath will disgust and frighten away the angels." She happened to have the best of it, however, for she quickly parried the blow by the reply: "Bless you, honey, I specs to leave dis bref behind when I goes to de angels."

Of all the men who need reforming, we would especially recommend for worthy consideration and for the prayers of a Christian people, our ministers, our

D.D.s, and our lecturers on temperance, who, in the least degree, are addicted to the use of tobacco. No man who is a moderate smoker has the right to preach against moderate drinking. Any man, whatsoever his station in life, who uses tobacco, forfeits his right and weakens his power to raise his voice against tobacco's companion. Alcohol and tobacco are twin demons. Temperance men, you cannot cure a drunkard while he is a slave to his pipe. Leading physicians claim that one artificial appetite generates another. True, every smoker and chewer of the filthy weed is not a drinker of intoxicants, but instances are very rare where the drunkard is not a slave to tobacco. As Horace Greeley once remarked: "Show me a drunkard who does not use tobacco, and I will show you a white blackbird." But little good can a minister do in preaching a gospel of purity and self-denial while he indulges in the use of the filth. In a certain theological seminary in Chicago, among the instructors, there are four out of seven, all D.D.s, who use tobacco. These are the men who are teaching our young men, by precept and example, to go forth and proclaim the *sweet, pure truths* of the gospel. Selah!!

We know of a young man who applied to this seminary for admission, but, on learning the fact just stated, he was so shocked that he left at once and took the course at another seminary in the same city; thus being obliged to change his denominational preference. For our part, we would not knowingly listen to an expounder of the teachings of Christ when those teachings came through such a dirty channel. We would prefer to worship under our own vine and fig-tree. You will observe that we adopt the motto we would have *all* men adopt; viz., *Feel not the public pulse to see if it beats in unison with yours.* God despises a coward. As you would strike straight from the shoulder, physically, so you should strike straight morally.

After lecturing on this subject in a certain church in Iowa, the pastor stepped forward, when the following colloquy took place:

"Mr. Warman, I am pleased to have you express yourself so freely and so forcibly on the care of the body, but *I* would not dare to do it."

"Have we not spoken the truth?"

"Ay, every word is true as gospel."

"Then, my brother, is it not logical to conclude that you dare not speak the truth?"

"Ah, but my bread and butter would be at stake."

"Then, for God's sake, and for humanity's sake, take the bread and let the butter go. We would rather live on a dry crust and carry about with us the sweet consciousness of being true to our convictions than to live in clover, and have bread, butter and honey."

It is not our desire to interfere with any one's liberty, only to draw a line on that liberty. His lordship may, at his own home, fill the house from cellar to garret with fumes of the weed, and no one object, unless it be his wife, and we would ask her if she remembers when, in years agone, she said, "No, sir, smoking is not objectionable;" but we cannot understand how men can be so selfish, and lack so much of the chivalric spirit for the fair sex that they will put ladies to any amount of discomfort, and thus satisfy their own selfish desires, by insisting upon the liberty to smoke in public places. We rejoiced to read upon a street car in Cincinnati the following order: "Smoking is prohibited upon any part of any car of the Cincinnati street-car lines."

If you will not count the cost as regards health and morals, then give a moment's consideration to the subject financially, and see what an expensive luxury it is.

Three 5-cent cigars daily for five years, with 6 per cent. compound interest semi-annually, amounts to $313.95.

Three 5-cent cigars daily for fifty years, with 6 per cent. compound interest, semi-annually, amounts to $16,236.37. When a man, at the age of seventy, has saved the snug little sum of $16,000, and it is his misfortune to lose it by fire, how he mourns; but what of the thousands of men around us who, from twenty to seventy, have deliberately sat down and *enjoyed* seeing the smoke of their $16,000. True, it was only a nickel or a dime at a time. These are facts—"stubborn facts," and figures never lie—except in election returns.

The burning of the filthy weed is but a small item when compared with the destruction of mind, body and morals. In your school-rooms, in your churches, in your offices, in your shops, in your public halls, in your hotels, in your theological seminaries, ay, in your pastor's study, we would have you hang up, in

the most conspicuous place and made in the most
attractive manner, the motto found in first Corinthians,
third chapter and seventeenth verse.

Here is missionary work for the good sisters. They
need not go to foreign lands; in many cases they need
not go from the shelter of their own homes.

We fear you will begin to think you are listening to
a dissertation on tobacco, instead of physical training,
but, considering the care of the body, we attack it
because it is such a powerful enemy. Then let us
entreat you, as you value your soul, your body, your
influence and the world's happiness, abandon the habit
if formed, and if not, avoid it; live and die with a
clean mouth, a sweet breath, a steady nerve, and a
clear conscience.

We trust we have mentioned sufficient results arising
from the use of this poisonous weed to set young men
and young women to thinking. Young women? Yes,
young women. We can point you to scores of cases
where young men have been encouraged in smoking because young ladies have said that it looked
manly.

We cannot imagine how a young lady of culture
and refinement, or of any delicacy whatsoever, can
press her pure lips to those of an habitual tobacco
chewer. She may possibly summon up courage
enough to do it before marriage, as she may have an
object in view—hopes to reform him; but after marriage we are inclined to think she will offer her *cheek*
instead of her *lips*, and in some cases it would take a
pretty *strong* cheek to do that. "Twere better to

*in*form him *before* marriage than to try to *re*form him *after* marriage.

The effect of tobacco upon the voice is also very injurious. It destroys the higher and purer tones. Our tenor singers are fast disappearing in consequence thereof.

One word more and we will leave the subject, strong as it is. There is scarcely anything from which we may not realize some good; so with tobacco. If any one is preparing to go as a missionary among the Cannibals, let him console himself, if he is an habitue of tobacco, that he will be perfectly safe with them, for they will not eat a man whose system is saturated with the vile stuff. They show good taste. And yet, we are brought to a halt, for this pernicious habit may not save one, after all, for they probably do their carving before they eat, and this would be too late to do one any good. We have met men, however, who, we think, would be perfectly safe, unless the Cannibal were exceedingly lively, for the acute olfactory of the latter would give him warning as to the kind of animal he was approaching.

We suppose that a first-class Cannibal, coming from one of the first-class families, would prefer to smoke his own meat.

Let us impress upon you, whatever may be the sin you are committing against your body, this thought: *Do not do that which you know to be hurtful, thinking that you may escape the penalty. Nature is unrelenting, and there is no vicarious atonement for sins against her.* Nature sets her mark of disapproval on all who disobey her.

We would establish one law—whether of the body or of the mind, whether it is in the form of pleasure or of physical exercise; *i. e.*, it should be encouraged or discouraged according as its effects are beneficial or otherwise to the health and to the morals.

TO SECURE LONGEVITY.

Alternate mental effort with some pleasant physical pastime. There is no one in any occupation who cannot find an opportunity, between the hours of rising and retiring, for at least a few moments exercise. When the brain is overtaxed, do something to draw the blood to other portions of the body. There is nothing gained by too steady mental application, for the mind needs rest, and nature demands it; and unless one yields to the demand, he will lose time in trying to collect and concentrate his thoughts. A change in the *line* of thought is also essential, for endless monotony will wear the fiber of any mind. The human body is like an engine; it will suffer a great amount of wear and tear with but *little* care, but with *proper* care the body may be so strengthened and the mind so disciplined, that we may live to the time allotted to man, "threescore and ten, and if by reason of strength they be fourscore years," etc., thereby admitting they may be fourscore, if, by reason of strength. Such we believe to be the purpose of the All-wise concerning every healthful child. How important, then, that parents and teachers see to the proper physical training of the children, that they may all reach to that good old age. Many a man lives out his days before he has time to fulfill the promise of his youth. According to the rules of the late Professor Faraday, the natural age of man should be one hundred years. The duration of life, both in man and animal, he believed to be measured by his time of growth, its natural termination being at five times that age, or five removes from that point. Man, being twenty years in growing, lives five times twenty, or one hundred years. He also divides life into two equal halves, growth and decline; and these two into infancy, youth, virility and age; infancy extending to the twentieth year; youth, to the fiftieth, because it is the period the tissues become firm; virility, from fifty to seventy-five, during which the organism remains complete, and at seventy-five old age commences.

Another eminent scientist, Dr. Farr, also says that the natural lifetime of a man is a century, which is the length of time the body will live under the most favorable conditions. Dr. Farr has divided life as follows: boyhood, ten to fifteen years; youth, fifteen to twenty-five years; manhood, twenty-five to fifty-five; maturity, fifty-five to seventy-five ; ripeness, seventy-five to eighty-five; and old age, eighty-five and upward.

There seems to be considerable doubt, however, as to whether the age of one hundred is at all near the limit to which people may and frequently do live. On this point Prof. J. R. Buchanan writes as follows, in the *Journal of Man:*

"The attainable limits of human longevity are generally underrated by the medical profession, and by public opinion. Instead of the Scriptural limit of threescore and ten, I would estimate *twice* that amount, or one hundred and forty years, as the ideal age of healthy longevity, when mankind shall have been bred and trained with the same wise knowledge that has been expended on horses and cattle.

"The estimate of one hundred and forty years as a practical longevity for the nobler generation is sustained by the number of that age (fourteen if I recollect rightly) found in Italy by a census under one of the later Roman emperors; but, for the race now on the globe, a more applicable estimate is that of the European scientist, that the normal longevity of an animal is five times its period of growth. Man's growth, however, is not limited to twenty ; and if we extend the period of maturity to twenty-eight, the same rule would give one hundred and forty as an age for the best specimens of humanity, and as this has been done in some cases, its general possibility, in improved conditions, is thus demonstrated."

Prof. Buchanan then gives a number of instances of persons *now* living who have nearly attained the age of one hundred and forty. Even if we *do* live to be one hundred and forty, we can consider that we have been cut off in the flower of our youth when compared with Methuselah and some others of his day.

Many of the pupils and friends of the writer will recall what he has so often said to them concerning his belief as to his own future; *i. e.*, that he fully expects to live to be one hundred years old, and furthermore, he does not intend to be in any one's way.

Such, friends, is our earnest belief; for we think if

by reason of strength it may be fourscore years, then by reason of more strength and proper care it may be extended to five score.

"What we sow, we shall reap." It is a very bad theory to teach young men that they must of necessity sow wild oats; but rather teach them that if they do, they must of necessity reap such a harvest.

Is there no need of any one being ill? No, not if he comes into the world a healthful child. He should pass through youth, manhood and old age, and not know an ache or a pain, unless the result of accident, or of extreme exposure, as was the case with many of us in the army. When he does go to the beautiful beyond, the house in which he has lived so long—having fully served its purpose—crumbles to dust, and the spirit takes its flight.

Is the writer never ill? He has been in years agone, but never expects to be again. 'T were better to say he never *will* be. All illness is a violation of some law of nature. For every violation of an ethical law you must pay a penalty ; so with every violation of the physical law you must yield to nature's unrelenting demands. Every ache or pain we have ever had has been traceable to some carelessness on our part, or unavoidable exposure.

We should be like the smooth rock upon the prairie; the winds may blow and lodge seed thereon, but if there is no soil it cannot take root; and so should it be with us. A germ of disease may be floating in the air, and it lodges upon a delicate and sensitive throat; it finds congenial soil, takes root and develops, and the doctor calls it diphtheria. Keep the body perfect by obeying nature's laws, and you can stand up in the midst of these floating germs and say, "I defy you to do me harm, for I have no congenial soil for your lodgment and development." Ah, but some one may raise the question, "Do you not think illness is providential?"

No, a thousand times, no; we have no doubt that it greatly displeases the Almighty when he beholds the weakness and folly of His children. He may *suffer* it, but we most emphatically say we do not believe that He *wills* it. Were it so, it would be an open rebellion against Him to take medicine for restoration, and every physician would be an enemy to His divine will.

Not long since, as we passed out of church on a Sabbath evening, our attention was drawn to an object which disgraced the title of man. He was one of the leaders, a pillar in the church—a rotten pillar, for he had so defiled the temple of God that his whole system was warped. We could scent the animal fifteen or twenty feet away. Think of that man in his home, or rather, think of his wife and children when shut up with that thing, and obliged to inhale the impure air caused by the poisoned emanations from his foul body. Suppose that man were taken ill. He calls himself a Christian, in consequence of which he would arrive at the *usual* conclusion, and consider his illness one of the dispensations of Providence, and he would bow submissively to the "will of God." (???) Shame on such a man for such blasphemy! His degraded condition was brought about by his own hand. He should also have a care not to heap too much of his guilt, even upon the devil. Our sympathy is sometimes aroused for His Satanic Majesty, as he often has to father much that does not belong to him.

Some years since, Henry Ward Beecher was called upon to visit a family, all of whom were ill. The good sister said: "Brother Beecher, I suppose it is the will of Him who knoweth best." Scarcely were the words uttered ere she met with the just reproof from her pastor, "It's no such thing; it's that stinking cabbage in your cellar."

DEGENERACY OF MAN.

Let us call your attention for a moment to man as he came from the hand of God. The late Hon. Horace Mann, in his dedicatory address as President of Antioch College, as far back as 1853, gave utterance to these memorable words: " I hold it to be morally impossible for God to have created in the beginning such men and women as we find the human race in their physical condition now to be.

" Examine the book of Genesis which contains the earliest annals of human history. With childlike simplicity this book describes the infancy of mankind. Unlike modern histories, it details the minutest circumstances of social and religious life; indeed it is rather a series of biographies than a history. The false delicacy of modern times did not forbid the mention of whatever was done or suffered, and yet over all that expanse of time, for more than a third part of the duration of the human race, not a single instance is recorded of a child born blind, or deaf, or dumb, or idiotic. During the whole period not a single case of a natural death in infancy, or childhood, or early manhood, or even in middle manhood, is to be found; not one man or woman died of disease. The simple record is, "And he died," or "He died in a good old age, and full of years," or "He was old and full of days." No epidemic or even endemic disease prevailed, showing that they died the natural death of healthy men, and not the unnatural death of distempered ones.

"Through all this time (except in the single case of Jacob in his old age, and then only for a day or two before his death), it does not appear that any man was ill, or that any old lady or young lady ever fainted. Bodily pain from disease is nowhere mentioned. No cholera infantum, scarlatina, measles, small-pox, not even a toothache. So extraordinary a thing was it for a son to die before his father, that an instance of it is deemed worthy of special notice, and this first case of the reversal of nature's law was two thousand years after the creation of Adam. See how this *reversal* of nature's law has for us become *the* law: for how rare it is now for all the children of the family to survive the parents. Rachel died at the birth of Benjamin, but this is the only case of puerperal death mentioned in the first twenty-four hundred years of sacred history, and even this happened during the fatigues of a patriarchal journey, when passengers were not wafted along in rail-car or steamboat.

"Do you think that Adam had tuberculous lungs? Was Eve flat-chested, or did she cultivate the serpentine line of grace in a curved spine? Did Nimrod get up in the morning with a furred tongue, or was he tormented with dyspepsia? Had Esau the gout or hepatitis? Imagine how the tough old patriarchs would have looked if asked to subscribe for an asylum for lunatics, or an eye and ear infirmary, or a school for idiots and deaf-mutes. What would their eagle vision and swift footedness have said to the establishment of a blind-asylum, or an orthopedic establishment? Did they suffer any of these revenges of nature against false civilization? No. Man came from the hand of God so perfect in his bodily organs, so defiant of cold and heat, of drouth and humidity, so surcharged with vital force, that it took more than two thousand years of the combined abominations of appetite and ignorance; it took successive ages of outrageous excess and debauchery, to drain off his electric energies and make him even accessible to disease; and then it took ages more to breed all these vile distempers which now nestle like vermin in every organ and fiber of our bodies.

"During all this time, however, the fatal causes were at work which wore away and finally exhausted the glorious and abounding vigor of the pristine race.

"After the exodus, excesses rapidly developed into diseases. First, came cutaneous distempers—leprosy, boils, elephantiasis, etc.,—the common effort of nature to throw visceral impurities to the surface. As early as King Asa, that right royal malady, the gout, had been invented. Then came consumptions and the burning ague and disorders of the visceral organs and pestilences—or, as the Bible expresses it, 'Great plagues and of long continuance, and sore sicknesses and of long continuance,' until, in the time of Christ, we see how disorders of all kinds, had become the common lot of mankind by the crowds that flocked to him to be healed ; and so frightfully and so disgracefully numerous have diseases now become that, if we were to write down their names in the smallest legible hand on the smallest bits of paper, there would not be room enough on the human body to paste the labels."

Let us start, as it were, in a new life, with a determination to fight those maladies that have settled upon us; let us obey the laws of health in every way that our reason may dictate; let us have, at all times, a plentiful supply of that which is so plentifully given, fresh air, even in the coldest weather. A person may live for days without food, but to deprive him of air, even for a few moments, would be to deprive him of life itself. *Breathe deeply.* Very few people do this as much as they should.

As to the matter of clothing, dieting and bathing, there can be no specific rules laid down to meet individual cases, as the same regime cannot well be provided for every one. Each one should be his own physician. Read, observe, think, and then wisely act.

We will, however, give a few of the

GENERAL RULES OF HEALTH.

Fresh air, cleanliness, wholesome food, exercise and

sleep are necessary for building a healthy body. If "cleanliness is next to godliness," good air is only second in importance to wholesome and sufficient food. There is an analogy between the rain descending on the parched earth, giving life to the fruits and flowers; and the blood coursing through the veins, renewing the wasted tissues of the body. The rain dissolves the chemical compounds in the earth, and shapes them to be absorbed by the rootlets of the growing plants. In like manner the blood carries nutrition to the body, and in itself furnishes food and deposits it particle by particle, thus building up the muscles, the teeth, the hair. the finger nails—in fact, every part of the human frame. The food must be ample and wholesome, to be readily transformed by the digestive apparatus into blood. The supply must be ample, and the quality pure and untainted. This material, from which only blood and bone is made, is conveyed to the heart. from there to the lungs, then into the heart again, and then through the arteries to the rootlets or capillaries, where it is used in building up the body. The passages of the blood through the heart and lungs is one of the wonders of the human organism. Good food makes good blood, but in a single circuit of the body, thousands of little pores are depositing into this pure stream of life, poisonous matter, dead particles from the system. This blood goes into the heart, thus charged. The heart then sends it into the lungs, and here is the great *filterer*. The lungs expose the dark colored blood to the action of oxygen from the air; the carbonic-acid gas, which is largely the air formed from decayed animal tissue, takes the place of oxygen in the lungs, and is thrown out by respiration. The purified blood returns to the heart a brilliant red, and starts on a fresh circuit to replace the dying tissues. How quickly the blood would clog the circulation and the heart cease to beat if the oxygen of the air failed to reach the lungs. The carbonic-acid gas (and other impurities exhaled from the lungs) is a poison. The air absorbs and dilutes this poison.

If for any reason the same air had to be taken into the lungs several times, death would ensue; the lungs would labor in vain to find the oxygen needed to renew the blood.

The assertion that every seven years the human body will have changed; that, particle by particle, the old will die and be replaced by new, is a form of the statement of the well-known truth that the exhalations of the body are continually depleting the system and as continuously is new matter substituted. This action is external as well as internal.

We have followed the blood in its circuit, and found it charged with impurities. We shall find by a microscopic examination that the million of pores in the skin are at work discharging the impurities from the body. These impurities largely pass into the air, to be taken into the lungs if the air is confined and breathed again. If, by the stoppage of the pores of the skin, this discharge of impurities is prevented, serious consequences at once result.

FRESH AIR.

A dearth of fresh air is of as great moment as a dearth of fresh water. Air twice breathed contains enough carbonic-acid gas to extinguish a light. Consider the fact that each individual should have two thousand cubic feet of fresh air every hour, and you will readily perceive the necessity of perfect ventilation. During the night sessions of schools and entertainments, it is even more difficult to receive a sufficient supply of oxygen; for every burning gas jet consumes as much oxygen as sixteen people.

On the 3d of February, 1857, the late Henry Ward Beecher, addressing an assemblage of New York medical students, gave utterance to the following: "The principal use which men seem to put air to is to destroy it. They go into their homes and shut out the exterior air, and burn by stoves that which is inside, and poison it by breathing, and then, when it is utterly destructive, go on breathing it and sucking it in as if it were a confection or a luxury. Is there anybody that teaches men what air is when applied to travel in steamboats? It is enough to set one to retching just to remember the cabin. Is there nobody to teach the community the benefit of air in railroad cars, in churches, in lecture halls, in places of crowded assemblies? We should scorn, with ineffable scorn, to sit down at a plate where a man had just eaten his meal, and take the fork or spoon that had just been in his mouth and put it in ours; but we will sit down and breathe the air that he has breathed, and that his wife has breathed, and that his children have breathed, and that the servants have breathed, and that forty others have breathed, and think it just as good for our breathing, and will breathe it over and over again as if it were a precious morsel. There seems to be no power to impress men that God made pure air for promoting health, and that impure air produces the crime of sickness, for I think that sickness is a sin."

CORRECT BREATHING.

Not only is it essential to have fresh air, but it is quite as essential for health to know how to use it, or breathe it. We all naturally breathe, but we do not all breathe naturally—that is, as nature intended. We should take, generally, but seventeen to twenty inhalations in a minute, but the majority of people, not breathing sufficiently deep, take about thirty inhalations a minute. The fact of the matter is, very few people know the real pleasure of living. They only *exist*, and drag out a *miserable* existence at that.

It is against all physiological law to practice *clavicular* breathing; that is, upper chest instead of the diaphragmatic. We have dwelt so fully on this subject in our book entitled, "Warman on the Voice," that it is not practical to deal with it here. We will pause, however, to speak of the matter of breathing as regards the mucous membrane, the lining of the nose, throat, etc.

We do not believe in any one having catarrh, sore throat, bronchial or lung trouble. Correct breathing will have much to do with correcting these difficulties, and in a great degree will prevent them. *Do not breathe through the lips.* The dog is the only animal that possesses this right, and he holds a license from nature. The dog is given the use of the tongue, with its unnumbered pores, to serve the same office as the pores of the skin with us; that is, as an aid to respiration. The mechanical process of breathing, known as respiration, is simple, being an alternate enlargement and contraction of the lung cavity. By this motion the air is made to fill the lungs, the blood is purified, and the air, taking up the waste, worn-out matter from the blood, is then expelled. The membrane lining the air-cells of the lungs would, if joined and spread out, cover a surface of twelve square feet. It is this surface that the air must visit twenty times a minute; through these twelve square feet of membrane, oxygen must be absorbed, and carbonic-acid and vapor be expelled.

If you are unfortunate enough to get "the snuffles," —the forerunner of a cold in the head—take a brisk walk and persistently breathe through your nostrils. Do not let a little thing like that master you. If you have the catarrh, sore throat, elongated uvula, swollen tonsils, etc., we would again invite you to a careful perusal of our book, "The Voice." We will assure you that if you keep your mouth shut and follow our instructions you will preserve a heathful condition of the throat, nasal, and even ear passages.

You should be able to baffle catarrh, diphtheria, sore throat, and all kindred diseases.

Do not breathe through your mouth even when you are asleep. True, you cannot lie awake to become cognizant of the fact. Cleanse your teeth well just before retiring, and if you cannot keep your mouth shut in any other way, do as the Indians with their pappooses—*tie* the mouth shut. The Indian warrior sleeps, hunts, and even smiles with his mouth shut, and respires through his nostrils.

For the preservation of the teeth, also, this precaution of keeping the mouth shut should be heeded. The teeth require moisture to keep their surfaces in good working order. When the mouth is open the mucous membrane has a tendency to become dry, the teeth lose their needed supply of moisture, and then comes discoloration, toothache, decay, looseness, and final loss of teeth. It is an excellent thing, also, to keep your mouth shut—when you are angry.

In the army, we learned, from compulsion, to keep our mouth shut when sleeping, always closing the lips and the teeth firmly; for there were numerous little strangers creeping and running here and there, hungry little strangers, that were always curious to look down a Yankee's throat. The habit of closing the mouth, when once acquired, is not soon forgotten.

BATHING.

This is a delicate subject to handle publicly. Some people are afraid of water, whether warm or cold. Cold water should be avoided at any time that the vitality is too low for reäction.

As for ourselves, we prefer a daily hand bath of cold water and sea-salt. Rock-salt or even table-salt will answer, but the sea-salt is preferable. We say a *hand* bath, because we prefer the warmth and magnetism of the hand to a glove, brush or sponge.

A handful of salt in a basin of water, about half full, will dissolve in a short time. These hand baths should follow some kind of physical exercise, and then once a week a hot-water bath, with soap, should be used in place of the salt bath. It were well to retire after the warm-water bath, as there will be less danger of taking cold; besides the complexion will be benefited by keeping warm after the bath. Should you, however, be obliged, directly after the warm-water bath to go into the open air, we would advise you to remove the stopple from the bath tub, when you finish your warm-water bath, and turn on the cold water, using it quite freely by the use of the hands; first on the hands, then arms, face, chest, and finally on the entire body; then, on leaving the bath, place your feet, alternately, for a moment or so, under the stream of cold water. This will prevent you catching cold. Do not dress until you are perfectly dry. The free use of salt water will prevent your face and hands from chapping. Salt water as a bath, salt water as a gargle, salt water for the nostrils, salt water for the hair, salt water for the eyes; by this time you will be so well salted that, paradoxical as it may seem, you will keep ever fresh.

CATARRH.

In the use of salt water for the nostrils, a douche should be employed. *Never snuff any liquid through the nostrils for the cure of catarrh*, for in so doing the

Eustachian tube will be opened and the liquid entering therein may cause deafness.

We will prescribe a remedy for catarrh. This prescription will cost but a few cents, but a Chicago doctor charges twenty-five dollars for it. It is very simple, but we have known it to be efficacious. " Dissolve one ounce of borax in one quart of rain-water and—" here we stop a moment, because said doctor advised the patient to snuff it "and not to use a douche." His objection to the douche was that the *force* is too great. We would say, remove the objection by not placing the douche high enough to create undue force. We believe that no liquid should ever be snuffed through the nostrils, because, as we said in the foregoing, it will enter the Eustachian tube, leading to the ears. The catarrh may thus be cured, but its cure may be purchased at the expense of the hearing. We will say, use a douche; and while the liquid is passing through the nostrils, hum the letter *M* on a high key. This closes the tube and prevents any further difficulty. Have the water tepid, as it will more readily allay the inflammation than if it were cold.

THE THROAT.

Do not muffle up your throat when winter comes. Nature does not need the precaution, but if used she will resent the removal of it. The protection of your throat rests in keeping your mouth shut, thus protecting the *lining* of the throat. The back part of the neck, also, should be protected, especially from draughts. If the barber wets your hair in winter, see that the back part of the head, especially back of the ears, is perfectly dry ere you change from the warm to the cold air. As with the throat, so with the chest, the caution is usually misapplied. An erroneous notion prevails that if only the chest is well protected from cold, no harm will ensue. Extra warmth is necessary at the *back*, over the situation of the chain of nerves known as the sympathetic, whose purpose it is to regulate the supply of blood to the various organs of respiration and digestion, and to keep those organs in co-ordination.

It is, undoubtedly, by draughts on the back of the neck, that colds, or inflammation due to colds, whether of the neck, chest or loins, are most frequently taken. See that your *chest* protector is a *back* protector.

The necessity of frequent bathing and change of underclothing is evident, from the fact that through the perspiratory glands of the skin is exhaled forty ounces of vapor each day; this vapor being loaded with the waste and impure matter which the lungs cannot remove. *Do not wear any undergarment at night which has been worn during the day.* It contains the excretions of the body, and will be reäbsorbed by the system. By all means

TAKE CARE OF THE FEET.

Avoid wearing rubbers at all when indoors, and wear them as little as possible at any time. They retain the waste matter of the system until reäbsorbed, and thus the blood becomes laden with impurities and poisons.

The feet should be kept dry. If they perspire freely the hose should be changed once or twice a day, especially if one is subject to or catches cold easily. Nervous, excitable people are very prone to clammy, cold, damp feet. People say that their feet perspire, but it is not really a perspiration, nor is it increased at all by warmth, but rather by the cold. It is, rather, the result of a very wakeful condition; and the excretion may be said to be the product of the worn out brain and nerves. It is always worse when the mind is most excited. Public speakers, singers and actors suffer much from it, and it predisposes them to catch cold. It troubles least when idling and quiet. A few minutes sleep will at any time dry up the soles made clammy by excitement. This ought to show that the feet do not perspire from the heat. There is no greater folly than to choose light cotton socks instead of woolen, to prevent this, as if it were a real perspiration.

Clammy feet are a common cause of sore throat, large tonsils, catarrh, and all that class of troubles. Men often catch cold without knowing how, or being able to account for it. They go home after a day of mental excitement, with the soles of the feet clammy and damp, and they change their boots for slippers, still wearing the damp socks. One should never make such a change without putting on dry socks. Children are much healthier for going barefoot while the ground is warm. That draws the blood to the feet, and relieves the brain. There is no better tonic for the nerves. Even adults would profit thereby

But when the ground is cold, woolen socks and warm, dry feet are essential, especially to those prone to catarrhal troubles.

COLOR OF THE CLOTHING.

This is a subject of no little importance. Light-colored clothing is preferable to dark; but fashion reigns supreme, and it is a common saying, though *not* "worthy of all acceptation," "You may as well be out of the world as out of the fashion."

How odd it would look to see one dressed in light clothing in winter; yet there is no doubt that it is warmer than black. Black is warmer in summer and cooler in winter, while white, on the contrary, is warmer in winter and cooler in summer. This assertion will stand a thorough investigation.

Our philosophy is this: black, when exposed to the sun's rays, will draw and radiate the heat, and absorb the light; white reflects the heat, radiates it but slightly, but it transmits the light. It is the *light* of the sun, not the *heat*, that the human body needs.

The effect of the sun in summer, being so much stronger than in winter, the light or white clothing resists the intense heat, reflecting it *outwardly*. In winter, the sun having but little effect, and the heat coming as it does from the body, and being *needed* for the body, the light clothing reflects it *inwardly*. Dressing in black in summer is equivalent to living in a cave, though not so comfortable; for, though you remain in the sunlight, your body receives no light, but suffers from the heat. If you have a nice plat of grass that you wish to save from the scorching rays of the sun, cover it with white, and thus prove the foregoing assertion. You will prove it still more conclusively if you cover another plat with black, for you will destroy the grass as completely as if you had covered it with a marble slab.

Blue is a very desirable color, as it is soothing in its effect on the eyes, and soothing to the individual, when worn as clothing.

The science of chromopathy—healing with colors—is worthy of most careful consideration. The word has not yet found a place in our dictionaries. We remember when the blue-glass healing was all the rage; it was used indiscriminately; other colors were needed as well as blue. Red has ever been the life-giving color, the blood. Then fancy one suffering with paralysis taking a sun bath with the light penetrating blue glass! You may as well put him in a refrigerator. Such a subject needs the life-giving principle. He should take it red hot, not blue cold. When you get warm does not your skin have the glow of red? When you are cold do you not look blue—to say nothing of feeling blue?

Druggists know that there are medicines that are excitants; others that are the reverse. They should also know, that each medicine, according to its nature, would the better retain its power if kept in bottles or packages of an appropriate color.

But recently, we read an article advising the ladies to wear red veils; they were recommended by certain doctors as a protection for the eyes. They must have been oculists who recommended them for the sake of "home protection" and not for "*free* trade," but for an *abundance* of trade; for it is an indisputable fact that no color is more trying to the eye than red. Red curtains in the school-room, or in any room much occupied, are often the cause of much color-blindness. We knew a paper-hanger who was blind three weeks in consequence of hanging a room with a satin-finish paper, the predominating color being red.

Yellow is a color which, when subjected to the rays of the sun, has a point of excellence not common to any other color. It filters, from the rays of the sun, the chemical element that proves so destructive in intense heat. A yellow covering to the head is a preventive of sun-stroke; hence those of us who insist upon the foolish fashion of wearing a black hat—especially a high silk one—can counteract the tendency of the absorbing and radiating influence of the black by lining it with yellow, thus robbing it of its injurious effect upon the brain. This is also fully illustrated in the fact that until the last few years the photographer could not expose a negative to the slightest ray of *daylight*, but it must be chemically prepared by *gas-light* before it could be shown to the subject for examination. Now, these negatives can be finished entirely by daylight, provided the light is admitted through yellow glass.

MAGNETISM.

While we are a firm believer, through many practical and personal experiments, in magnetism, hypnotism, psychology, mesmerism, thought-transference, mental telegraphy, mind-reading, etc., it is our purpose, in these pages, to speak of magnetism *only as regards health*, and as best serves us in the care of the body.

All persons are more or less magnetic, differing in degree and kind. Some persons are absorbers, others imparters; some attract, others repel. There are many phases of magnetism; such as is needed by the public speaker in psychologizing his audience, or by the teacher in her schoolroom, or by the human being over the brute creation, etc.; but we must necessarily confine ourselves to the question of health-giving and health-receiving. We are never so positive or so negative as to neither give or take.

When one wishes to impart, he should sit facing the north, with the back of his subject to the north. The operator should sit a trifle higher than his subject. He should take the subject's hands in his and press his thumb either upon the median or ulnar nerve. Touch his knees to the knees of his subject, thus closing the current. This is sufficient to open the channel of magnetic communication.

It is not necessary to pass into the realm of mesmerism. By taking this position, and following the brief instructions here given, one of greater strength may readily give of his or her magnetic power to a weaker one. Like two canal locks, side by side, the one full of water, and the other empty, if the gate is opened between them, the result will be equilibrium.

Do not delude yourself with the idea that because

you can hold the poles of a battery for a long while, you are much more magnetic than your friend who drops them much sooner. The reverse is true. Lightning does not strike a dead tree. The *less* life you have, the more *need* of the life-giving principle—electricity; while the one who is *full* of life may soon become *surcharged*. Remember, also, that electricity and magnetism are not synonymous terms. You can insulate electricity, but you cannot insulate magnetism.

If you are sitting with another, and you desire to load up with magnetism, do not fail to get on the right side of him or her, *i. e.*, the right-hand side. Most thoroughly have we demonstrated the fact that we take magnetism into the left side, and give it out at the right side, if there is any one at the right to receive it; if not, we retain it.

When a young man and a young lady go out riding, the lady should sit on the *right* side of him, and our word for it, she will perceive a change in the matter of strength which she has not previously experienced on similar occasions. She may think the air has more electricity than usual, or that she is being benefited by the animal magnetism of the horse, but, if she is honest, she will admit that it is all due to the exhilarating influence of the man who sits beside her, though he may be wholly unconscious of the good he is doing, unless a feeling of "goneness" seizes him—after she has gone.

This now brings us to the consideration of a subject in which we all have much interest.

SLEEPING AT WILL.

You should be a thorough master of yourself. You should so thoroughly understand every part of your organism that you know how to place yourself in a condition to *impart* strength when you are *surcharged* with it, or to *receive* it when you are in *need* of it.

This is of especial importance as pertains to sleep. You should be able to go to sleep, within two minutes, at any time of the day or night, even under trying circumstances. It is a mistake to wait until nature calls for rest, for, unless it be force of habit in retiring at a particular time, it is an indication of undue expenditure of either mental or physical force. Study the law of equilibrium and centralization. It is the law of the universe. You cannot expect to retire and sleep sweetly when your brain is too active. There is an excess of blood there, and you should take some physical exercise to draw the blood to some other portion of the body. Rise slowly on your toes, from forty to one hundred times, and thus draw the blood to your limbs; you will find immediate relief, especially at the base of the brain. The doctors say, some of them, that if you cannot sleep, get up and eat, and give the stomach something to do. They probably mean, give the *doctors* something to do. It is all right to eat when you are hungry, provided the appetite is a natural one. A foot bath every night in hot water will be found conducive to sleep. Cold water drives the blood to the brain, but if one has considerable vitality, the reaction is quick, and will result in producing the same effect. On the whole we would, however, recommend the hot water, especially if you are troubled with cold feet. Some of us, with remarkably strong constitutions and perfect circulation, complain (?) of cold feet—but they are not *ours;* they belong to the better-half—the half that is never benefited by any amount of exercise that we may take. If you are troubled with cold hands and feet, we will guarantee a more perfect circulation if you will follow our prescription: Place your feet in hot water; and around the neck, place a band of cloth dipped in *cold* water. When taking the feet out of the hot water, place them in cold water or dash cold water upon them. The band about the neck will check the flow of blood toward the head and will cause it to reäct, sending it to the hands and feet, thereby producing better circulation. We also strongly advise the use of magnetic insoles; in fact, any good magnetic garments, such as will revitalize the blood, and throw back into the system that vital force which would otherwise be lost.

In this matter of health and exercise each one is a law unto himself. Some of us can stand more work than others without overtaxing nature. It has not been an uncommon thing in our experience to be engaged in our little den all day, and until two or three o'clock in the morning, and this for months in succession, without feeling any weariness whatever. Should we feel the least symptoms of weariness and confusion of ideas, or lack of mental concentration, we would pause at once, even if in the middle of a word.

We make it a rule to leave our work on our desk—not to take it to bed with us—and though we do not feel, in the least, the need of sleep, we can go to sleep within two minutes after retiring. Do you want to possess the secret? You are welcome to it. When we have disrobed for the night—or morning—we swing a pair of Indian-clubs, then take a hand bath of salt and water, and in a few minutes thereafter we are quietly resting in the "arms of Morpheus" without the aid of morphine.

With some constitutions, cold water would make them wakeful; then we would recommend warm water, though it is not so strengthening.

We do not advocate late hours as a general thing, for, *cæteris paribus*, an hour of sleep before midnight is worth two hours after, owing to the change in the electric currents. Yes, we believe in having the head of the bed to the north, especially for those who are sensitive to the effects of currents of electricity.

If you do not sleep well, you should seek the cause. If you do not sleep *alone*, it may be due to the fact that your bedfellow is robbing you of your magnetism. The remedy is very simple—just sleep on the other side; no matter whether it is north, east, south or west—change *sides* and you will change the *conditions*.

Not long since a lady pupil said to us, "I have been feeling like a new creature since two years ago when I took your instruction. I gained in health and strength; but my energy, my ambition and my strength have all left me within a week or so, and I cannot account for it." On questioning the lady, with a view to the cause, we found that since her husband's absence she had been sleeping with a younger sister. We informed her that her sister, though strong and healthful, was unconsciously robbing her of her magnetism. We requested her to change sides with her sister, but to say nothing in reference to it. She said she would try it, but she laughed at the idea of that doing any good. We told her to try it just one night, and not to laugh until the next morning. Near noon of the next day we met her on the way to the post-office. She looked so happy, and tripped so lightly, that for a time we did not know whether it was a lady or a bit of sunshine floating along. She said, "Would you believe it? I feel once more like a new creature. But you ought to see my sister!" When she informed us that she had told her sister the cause, and informed her from whom she received the advice, we didn't have the slightest desire to meet that sister. Shortly afterward, we saw her coming, but we just happened to think of an errand in an opposite direction. Every sunshine must have its shadow, but we try to get away from the shadows. We knew the sister could stand it.

It is a well-established fact that it is better to lie on the right side, especially if there is undigested food in the stomach. A lawyer can lie—on either side. Lying on the right side is also less likely to crowd the heart, which should be free in its function. If you should awaken and find it hard to go to sleep again, take Benjamin Franklin's method; turn down the clothing, let the bed air, and walk about for a few moments.

If you wish to add years to your life, and life to your years, make it an invariable rule to take your daily siesta—your afternoon nap. You should never begin any mental or physical exercise directly after a meal. The digestive organs need the extra supply of blood. You can afford to take a siesta; you cannot afford to omit it, for it will cost you but fifteen minutes of time.

Do not lie down, as it will crowd the digestive organs so soon after the noon meal, but sit in an easy chair, that your head may rest easily; then place your feet in a comfortable position about the height of the chair on which you are sitting; cross your limbs at the ankles, clasp your hands together easily, close your eyes, and by thus completing the circuit you will fall asleep through this process of self-magnetism in less time than it takes us to give you the *modus operandi*. You may not do it the *first* time you try it, but it is bound to follow successive attempts. It is worth your effort, if it takes weeks. The fifteen minutes rest *without* the sleep will be greatly beneficial. Do not neglect the importance attached to the position of the feet. We learned this principle while in the army, but did not learn the philosophy of it until many years after. During the long, weary marches, unless we were after something—or something was after us—we usually had a rest of ten minutes in about every hour. It was the custom of the author to immediately loose his shoes, slip them off, and drop asleep, whether deep in the dust or deeper in the mud. This he did instinctively, without knowing why or wherefore. We have since learned that the feet go to sleep first, the brain last; hence the necessity of having the feet in as comfortable a position as possible. Have you not often demonstrated this truth when riding on the cars? How you have turned and twisted to get your feet comfortable, no matter if your head was in danger of being divorced from your body. Persevere in your efforts to gain your fifteen minutes siesta and you will never regret it. You will soon be able to sleep without being annoyed by such little things as excessive light, or excessive noise. If you have engagements at night—upon the rostrum, upon the stage, or at the sacred desk—after a fatiguing journey, or having been busy during the day, take your few minutes of rest just previous to your departure for the hall, theater or church. You had better have your rest than your food; take both if you can.

Lie flat on your back and breathe deeply forty or fifty times very slowly, but do not go to sleep in that position, and you will get up feeling like a new man. Did you ever observe a horse or a mule after a hard day's work when the harness has been removed? The animal instinct says, " Roll, roll over," and if he *does* go over (and the mule *always* does), you will find him quite ready for the harness again. Those of us in literary pursuits might often learn lessons of great profit from the brute creation.

BELT AND CORSET.

A word to the gymnast, base-ball player or workman as regards the use of a belt. He makes a serious mistake in drawing a belt tightly around him. He may fancy that it supports him; so it does, but just in the same way that the corset—we think if it were properly named it would be called the *curse-it*—supports the young lady. A belt or corset impedes respiration, compresses the muscles of the abdomen, subjecting them to unnecessary friction, and actually impedes motion. Any form of dress or belt that constrains the base of the lungs and presses upon the stomach and intestines must do serious harm. Corsets kill more than cannon. Only men are slain in war; nature keeps up the balance by allowing women to slay themselves. At a very early age, pride places these corsets and bands about the tender, delicate body of the school-girl. You would be shocked, horrified, if any one were to tell you that you had just placed a serpent around the waist of your little daughter; the serpent is unseen, but he draws tighter and tighter every year.

A slender waist, made so by a corset, is neither healthful nor beautiful, and only an ignorant mind or a perverted taste would ever regard it as such. We are pleased to note a few words from the pen of Olive Logan on this subject:

"Every one knows of the appearance of the pale mother with her puny babe, born after prolonged throes of which the Indian squaw is as ignorant as she is of the corset torture of civilized life. Free from the corset! Why, it should make your blood leap merrily through the veins merely to utter these words; and free from it, mark you, not only in the privacy of one's dressing room, but also relieved of its baleful influence and hurtful pressure when equipped for the promenade, or dressed for the drawing room. Let it once be understood that to wear one's natural waist is the highest fashion, and the venomous stay-lace will loose its hold on its last half-stifled victim. In London, the great firm of Hamilton & Co., Regent street, have taken what is a decided stand; *they fit no dresses over corsets;* in other words, they make garments for *human, feminine beings,* not for *dummies of steel and whalebone.*"

We often hear of women being "dressed to kill." How true the expression, but in a very different sense than is suggested. "'Tis pity 'tis, 'tis true," but it is a greater pity that others than themselves must suffer the death penalty. Not satisfied with committing *suicide* by slow degrees, they must entail misery upon coming generations, and too frequently add *murder* to suicide. Consider for a moment how many there are who yearly commit suicide, not in a moment of passion (which might be forgiven), or in a fit of insanity (which might be forgiven), but coolly, deliberately, and as Christian (???) men and women. How appalling the number! How like blasphemy to have these charged up to the Almighty by saying that "The Lord giveth and the Lord taketh away; blessed be the name of the Lord." The Lord gives us all certain privileges and He takes them away when we abuse His precious gifts. In other words, when we are placed on this earth, we are all put here with one proviso; we must conform to nature's laws or suffer the penalty, and blessed be the name of the Lord, those laws are immutable.

If in *heaven* there will be no one who has committed suicide, how crowded that *other* place will be!

Let us go back, just for a moment, to the corset. It is by no means an attractive subject, except by the law of association. It is only a waste-basket, with no poetry in it—though some men think them jewel cases. True, the corset is a hackneyed subject; so is temperance; and we must remember that temperance should be applied to *all* things. Are women temperate in the matter of corsets? Certainly. We never knew a woman who wore her corset tightly—*never;* that is, if we take her word for it; and what *can* we do but take her word? We would like to see the corset banished from the land, and to hasten that glad time we offer, gratuitously, two recipes, the use of which, we think, would be successful exterminators.

First, in reply to the familiar couplet so often quoted by the ladies:

> "The lips that touch wine
> Shall never touch mine,"

we would like to have our brothers reply:

> A woman—but no corset,
> For I can't indorse it;
> And not another embrace
> Till the corset you unlace.

Second, were the men to band themselves together and publicly declare that they would never again embrace a young lady who wore a corset—except on trial—ere the sun had descended on that proclamation, the corsets would part company with their victims to whom they had so fondly clung.

"On the score of health, the distorted feet of the Chinese, or the deformed skulls of the Flathead Indians, are less objectionable than the cramped waists of our devotees of fashion. As regards beauty, it is hard telling which infringes most upon a true ideal." What is beauty? Has physical exercise anything to do with it? Yes, in both face and form. There are no really *pretty* men, though the term is often misapplied. There are *beautiful* and *handsome* men and women, but *character* is one of the constituents. What is called a pretty man, is nothing more nor less than a suit of clothes, latest fashion, passing down the street without anything in it. No man or woman may be termed really beautiful before arriving at the age of forty or forty-five. There are very few handsome men and women. *Young* womanhood is beautiful in a soft, dreamy, day-dawn loveliness, but she never reaches her real beauty until womanhood has developed body, mind and soul, with the touches of thought, feeling, love, care and grand resolve.

The youth, just fledged as a professional man, must wait years until the lines of experience, close thought, professional conflicts, business excitement, hopes blasted and hopes realized have chiseled a few lines upon his face and the brilliancy of sobriety in his eye; then, if *pure*, he is beautiful.

SYMMETRICAL DEVELOPMENT.

Let us strive, then, for bodily and mental development; let us discipline the physical, side by side with the mental, but never let the one pass the other, and in this way each may be made to sustain the other, thereby producing our threefold aim, health of body, health of mind, and graceful carriage of the body. These three, when attained, will give us symmetrical development.

A gentleman's arm, even an athlete's, when pendant at the side and the muscles relaxed, should be as symmetrically beautiful as is the shapely arm of a perfectly developed woman. The same holds good of the entire body. There is not a portion of the body that cannot be fully developed by proper exercise and manipulation.

Observe those who *do* practice gymnastics in our public schools, and also athletes of more or less reputation, and you will see that many of them are stoop-shouldered and pass along the street in a careless, slip-shod, shuffling manner. "All exercises which do not tend to ease, dignity and grace of carriage, are of questionable utility." Exercise, if properly taken, and under proper influences, should give elasticity of step, buoyancy, firmness without rigidity, active chest, and a general ease and gracefulness.

In every town where it is our privilege to meet those interested on this subject, we would be pleased to aid them in the organization of a class in gymnastic exercises. It can easily be done, and it will be a benefit to the community, even though the class may, for quite a while, use nothing but the dumb-bells. It will be the nucleus from which grand results will be sure to follow.

If parents and educators throughout the land would

give us a helping hand by pushing forward the good work, aiding us by their watchfulness and care, ere long it would appear that an entirely new race of beings had sprung into existence, and our asylums and hospitals would become gymnasiums, and our boys and our girls would be the pride of our country.

We should not boast of freedom in this great land of ours, for we are all a race of slaves—slaves to some pernicious soul-destroying or body-destroying habit. Let us free ourselves from everything that impedes our progress toward the highest ideal of manhood and womanhood, in form, in character, and in health.

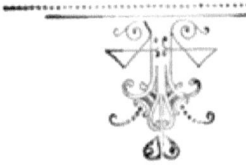

WARMAN'S
PHYSICAL EXERCISES WITHOUT APPARATUS.

Pure air, freedom of the muscles, and freedom of the joints are the first requisites toward physical training. Always breathe through the nostrils, and take deep inhalations to the waist. Do not allow the chest to rise and fall, however violent may be the exercise.

To increase the lung capacity, and to enable one to so develop the chest muscles that the chest may be raised and fixed by muscular action only—not by breathing—we prescribe the first three exercises.

THE LUNGS.

Place the hands on the chest, as shown in the illustration. Take a deep inhalation, and *retain* it while giving rapid but slight percussive blows with the fingers—not the palm of the hand. Continue the percussion while slowly counting four (mentally); expel the breath, but keep the arms in position during the entire exercise.

N. B. It is especially important that the elbows be kept on a line with the shoulders, as seen in the illustration.

Fig. I.

Hands—place.   Inhale—Percussion—Exhale.
      "   "   "   "
      "   "   "   "

THE CHEST.

Place the arms at the side, as shown in the illustration. Take a deep inhalation, and retain it during the exercise. Raise the hands slowly up and forward till they pass above the face and meet—the little fingers resting against each other. Draw the arms back to the side, as in starting; again forward, and again back before expelling the breath.

FIG. 2.

Hands—place. Inhale. Forward-Back-Forward-Back. Exhale.

THE SHOULDERS.

A SPECIAL EXERCISE FOR THOSE WHO ARE STOOP-SHOULDERED.

Place the arms at the side, as shown in the illustration. Take a deep inhalation, and retain it during the exercise. Pass the arms slowly forward till they are fully extended in a horizontal position, with all the muscles relaxed, the hands open—palms downward. Draw the arms slowly back to the side, as though *stretching* the muscles. The first impulse, on moving the arms back, should be felt at the elbow. Move them out straight from the shoulder, then down and back till the little fingers touch the ribs; again forward and again back, before expelling the breath

FIG. 3.

Hands—place.　Inhale.　Forward-Back-Forward-Back.　Exhale.

FREEDOM OF THE JOINTS.

THE FINGERS.

Place the arms as shown in the illustration. Put sufficient force in the fore-arms and hands to differentiate the fingers, while thrusting the hands up and down.

Take the life so completely out of the fingers as to remove all rigidity therefrom.

Continue these exercises but a few seconds at a time; but take them often.

FIG. 4.
Fingers—place.   Thrust............Rest.
               "   .... "
               "   "

THE WRISTS.

Place the arms at the side as shown in the illustration. Place sufficient force in the fore-arms to thrust the hands from side to side. Arrest the vitality at the wrist joints.

Continue these joint exercises but a few seconds at a time; but practice them quite often.

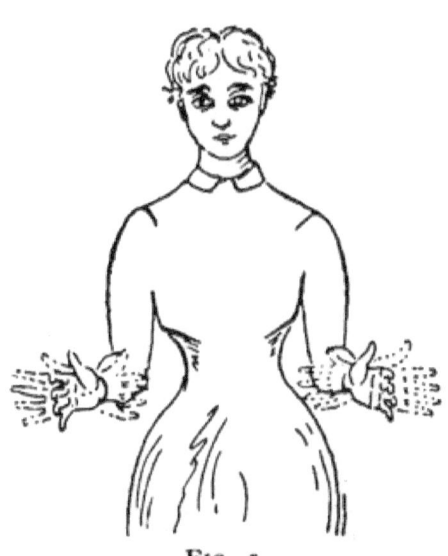

FIG. 5.

Wrists—place.   Thrust—in and out......Rest.
     "   "   "   " ...... "
     "   "   "   " ...... "

THE WRISTS.

Place the arms as shown in the illustration. Put sufficient force in the fore-arms to thrust the hands up and down.

As in the foregoing exercise, arrest the vitality at the wrist joints, and cease the exercise before it becomes tiresome, as these movements are especially intended for the joints, not the muscles.

FIG. 6.

Wrists—place. Thrust—up and down.......Rest.
    "   "   "   "   "   " ...... "
    "   "   "   "   "   " ...... "

THE WRISTS.

Place the arms as shown in the illustration. Put sufficient force in the fore-arms to whirl the hands inward. Imagine the hands lifeless—as if they were simply tied to the wrists.

Arrest the vitality at the wrist, and cease the exercise ere it becomes tiresome.

FIG. 7.

Wrists—place.   Whirl inward,......Rest.

THE WRISTS.

Place the arms as shown in the illustration. Put sufficient force in the fore-arms to whirl the hands outward. Imagine the hands lifeless—as if they were simply tied to the wrists. Arrest the vitality at the wrists, and cease the exercise ere it becomes tiresome.

FIG. 8.

Wrists—place. Whirl outward......Rest.
    "   "   ...... "
    "   "   "

THE ELBOWS.

Bend the body to the left, placing the left hand to the side, as shown in the illustration.

Raise the right arm till the elbow is even with the shoulder. Arrest the vitality at the elbow, thus causing the fore-arm and hand to hang lifeless from the elbow. Put strength in the upper arm, and move it backward and forward.

FIG. 9.

Elbow—right—place. Forward and backward..... Rest.
      "   "   "   ......   "
      "   "   "   ......   "

THE ELBOWS.

Bend the body to the right, placing the right hand to the side, as shown in the illustration. Raise the left arm till the elbow is even with the shoulder. Arrest the vitality at the elbow, thus causing the forearm and hand to hang lifeless from the elbow. Put strength in the upper arm, and move it vigorously backward and forward.

FIG. 10.

Elbow—left—place. Forward and backward....Rest.
"   "   "   ...."
"   "   "   ...."

THE SHOULDERS.

Take the life out of the entire arm—both arms; arresting all vitality at the shoulders.

Put sufficient strength in the chest to twist the body quickly by one impulse to the left, allowing both arms to sway freely; but bring the body back to position. Do not repeat the impulse till the arms have ceased swaying. Avoid rigidity of the arms.

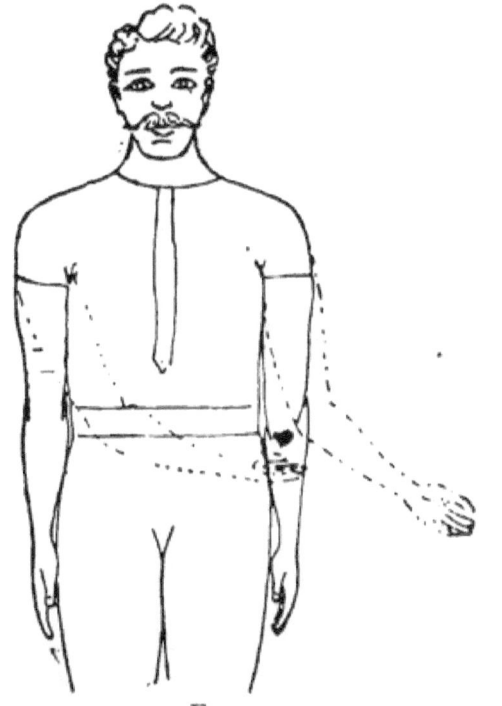

Fig. 11.
Shoulders. Impulse to the left—Position.
"   "   "   "   "
"   "   "   "   "

THE SHOULDERS.

Take the life out of the entire arm—both arms; arresting all vitality at the shoulders.

Put sufficient strength in the chest to twist the body quickly by one impulse to the right, allowing both arms to sway freely; but bring the body back to position. Do not repeat the impulse till the arms have ceased swaying. Avoid rigidity of the arms.

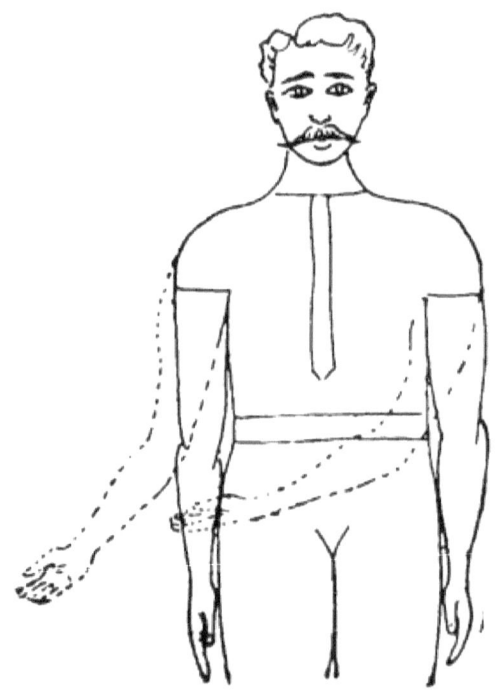

FIG. 12.
Shoulders. Impulse to the right—Position.
" " " "
" " " "

THE NECK.

Drop the head slowly toward the right side. Do not allow the body to sway or bend, or the head to turn. Let the head drop low enough and with sufficient force to strengthen the muscles of the opposite side of the neck. Raise the head slowly, and then drop it in the same manner toward the *left* side, observing the same instruction and caution as when dropping it toward the right.

Fig. 13.

Head. Right—Raise—Left—Raise.

THE NECK.

Drop the head slowly forward, and as low as possible—the lower the better, for strengthening the muscles of the neck; also for giving flexibility and ease to the various movements of the head. Keep the body firm in all the neck exercises. Raise the head slowly, and drop it in the same manner backward, allowing it to go as far back as possible in order to strengthen the muscles of the throat. Avoid all jerkiness.

FIG. 14.
Head. Forward—Raise—Backward—Raise.

THE NECK.

Drop the head slowly forward, and as low as possible. Roll it very slowly toward the right side; then as far back as possible; then to the left side, and forward to position.

FIG. 15.

Head. Forward—Right—Back—Left—Forward—Rest.
     "   "   "   "   "   "
     "   "   "   "   "   "

THE NECK.

Turn the head very slowly to the right until a perfect profile is formed; then back to position; then to the left, until a perfect profile is formed. Keep the head erect and the body firm—immovable.

FIG. 16.

Head. Right—Front—Left—Front.
" " " "
" " " "

THE WAIST.

STRENGTHENING THE BACK AND THE ABDOMEN.

Stand erect, with the weight of the body on both feet. Place the hands on the hips, as shown in the illustration. Bend slowly forward, and as low as possible, until feeling a strong tension at the small of the back, and along the back part of the limbs. Rise slowly to position, and bend backward as far as possible, without becoming unbalanced. Change the pressure of the fingers from the abdomen to the small of the back, as shown in the illustration. Rise slowly to position.

Caution.—Allow the limbs to bend at the knee in the backward motion, and refrain from laughing when in this position.

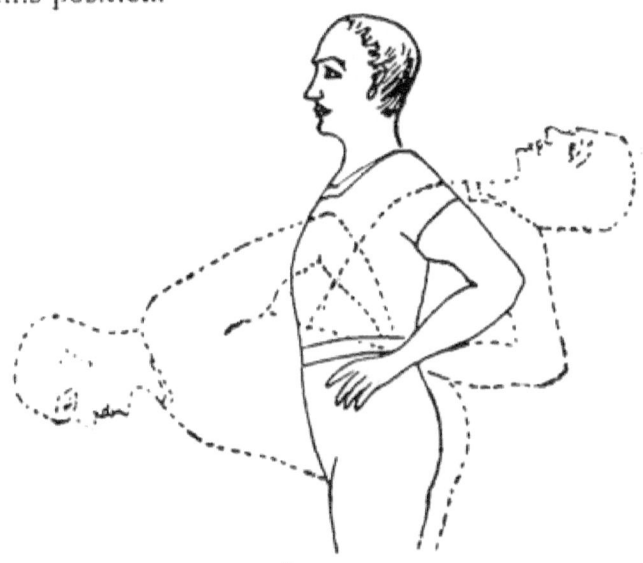

FIG. 17.

Waist. Place hands.
   Down up—change fingers—Back - up—Change.

THE WAIST.

RIGHT AND LEFT SIDE.

Place the hands upon the ribs, as shown in the illustration. Bend the body as far as possible to the left—without moving the right foot. Rise slowly, and bend the body as far as possible to the right—without moving the left foot. Pass slowly back to position. Bend as low as possible in each case; so low as to cause great tension of the muscles over the ribs on either side.

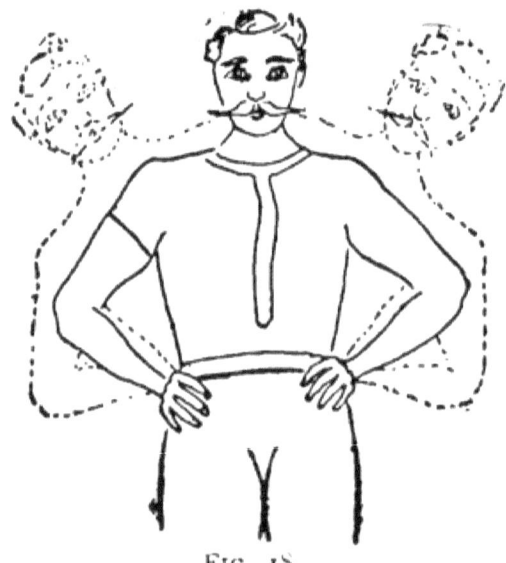

FIG. 18.

Waist. Place hands. Left—Up—Right—Up.
                         "   "   "   "
                         "   "   "   "

THE ENTIRE WAIST.

Stand erect. Place the hands on the side of the body—palms to the ribs. Turn or twist the body as far as possible to the right without moving the feet; then back to position; then as far as possible to the left, and back to position.

FIG. 19.

Waist.   Place hands.   Right—Front—Left—Front.

THE HIPS.

Place the hands on the hips. Stand erect, with the weight of the body on the left foot. Paw with the right foot by first drawing it well back, then raising the right knee quite high, and pushing the right foot forward. Allow the limb to fall quite heavily—the foot striking the floor.

FIG. 20.

Hips. Place hands. Paw. Back—Up—Down.

THE HIPS.

Place the hands on the hips. Stand erect, with the weight of the body on the right foot. Paw with the left foot by first drawing it well back, then raising the left knee quite high, and pushing the left foot forward. Allow the limb to fall quite heavily—the foot striking the floor.

Fig. 21.

Hips.   Place hands.   Paw.   Back—Up—Down.

THE KNEE.

Place the hands on the hips. Stand erect, with the weight of the body on the left foot. Raise the right foot till the calf of the limb presses against the thigh, as shown in the illustration. Place the foot to the floor noiselessly.

FIG. 22.

Knee. Place hands. Up—Down—Up—Down.

THE KNEE.

Place the hands on the hips. Stand erect, with the weight of the body on the right foot. Raise the left foot till the calf of the limb presses against the thigh, as shown in the illustration. Place the foot noiselessly to the floor.

FIG. 23.

Knee. Place hands. Up—Down—Up—Down.

THE ANKLE.

Place the hands on the hips. Stand erect, with the weight of the body on the left foot. Raise the right foot from the floor, and put sufficient strength in the limb to shake the foot.

FIG. 24.

Ankle. Place hands. Raise the foot—Shake—Rest.

THE ANKLE.

Place the hands on the hips, with the weight of the body on the right foot. Raise the left foot from the floor, and put sufficient force in the limb to shake the foot.

Fig. 25.

Ankle. Place hands. Raise the foot—Shake—Rest.
" " " " "
" " " " "

FOR THE MUSCLES.

THE CALF AND THIGH.

Stand erect. Rise slowly on the toes, raising the heels as far as possible from the floor. Poise a few seconds, then allow the heels to touch the floor, but do not sink heavily upon them, nor allow the body to sway backward and forward. Place the hands on the hips, as it will aid in maintaining a balance.

Fig. 26.

Place hands.   Rise on toes.   Up—Down—Up—Down.
        "   "   "   "
                      "   " from 10 to 50 times.

THIGHS.

Place the hands on the hips. Bend both knees, and settle the body toward the floor, sitting—or so endeavoring—upon the heels. Keep the body erect from the waist up. Spring up to position as soon as the lowest position is reached.

FIG. 27.

Sit. Place hands. Down—Up—Down—Up.
" " " "
" " from 10 to 25 times.

FORE-ARM.

Have the arms rest easily at the side, as shown in the illustration. Close the hands tightly, and open them vigorously, thrusting the fingers out and extending or stretching them as much as possible.

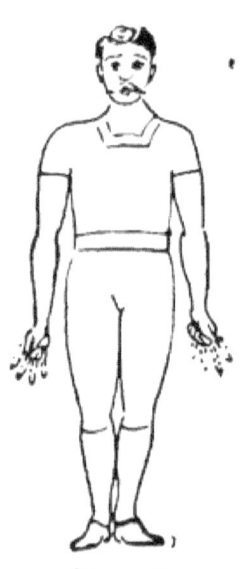

FIG. 28.

Fingers. Shut—Open—Shut—Open.
" " " "
" "   from 10 to 25 times.

CHEST AND ARMS.

Stand erect between two desks or chairs, or in front of a chair with high arms. Bend forward, and place the hands as shown in the illustration. Step back until only the toes touch the floor. Hold up the head so that the body is straight from head to foot. Let the body down slowly between the desks or chairs, or chair arms.

Let the body down as far as possible, then straighten the arms, raising the weight of the body, resting on them. Do not *beyd* the body, but keep it perfectly straight from head to foot.

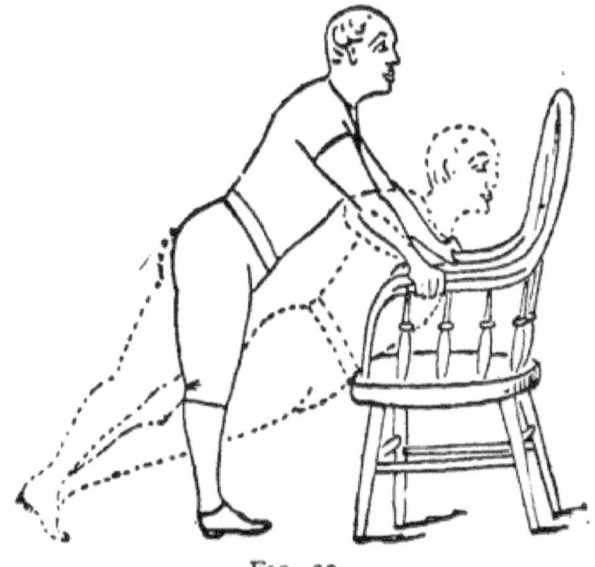

FIG. 29.

Chair.   Position—Hands—Feet.   Down—Up.

From 3 to 25 times.

NOTE.

If all the movements of the preceding exercises are taken, from three to five times will suffice, especially for school or class work.

Those persons having more time and desiring more rapid development, may increase the number of times of each movement to any extent that will not cause fatigue. The author generally takes each exercise about twenty-five times. Some of these are favorites. For instance, the exercise illustrated by Fig. 26 he always takes fifty times, at least; often increasing it to a hundred. After hours of mental labor, it is especially helpful in drawing the extra amount of blood from the brain to supply the muscles.

To this list of exercises without apparatus, may be added the dumb-bell system.

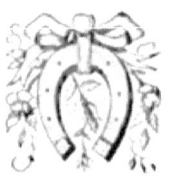

98 PHYSICAL TRAINING.

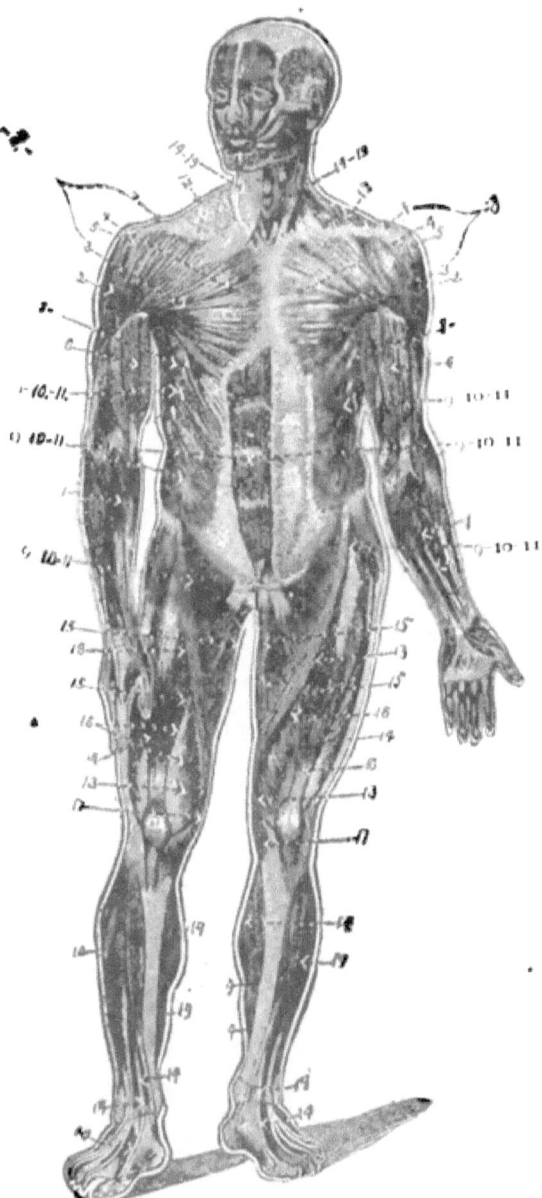

FRONT VIEW OF MUSCLES.

N. B.—By referring to page 100, you will find that the numbers used in the above figure correspond with the various exercises given in Warman's Dumb Bell System.

PHYSICAL TRAINING.

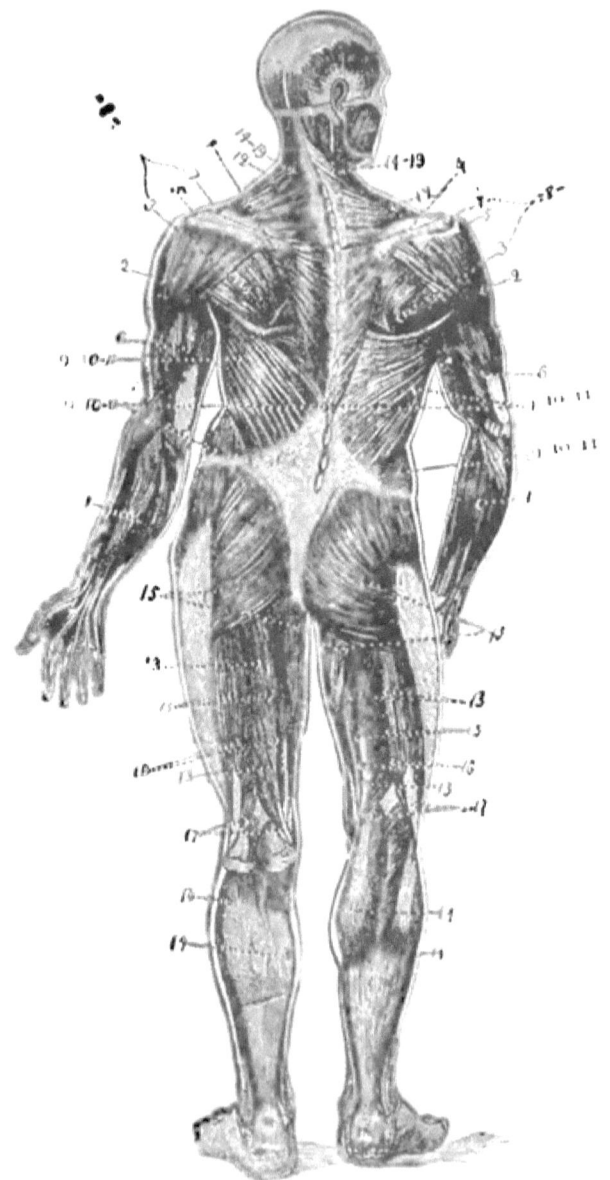

BACK VIEW OF MUSCLES.

N. B.—By referring to page 100, you will find that the numbers used in the above figure correspond with the various exercises given in WARMAN'S DUMB BELL SYSTEM.

WARMAN'S DUMB-BELL SYSTEM.

KEY TO THE PHYSIOLOGICAL CHART.

The figures on the charts correspond with those of the dumb-bell exercises; showing the muscles that are developed when the movements are taken as indicated by the chart figures.

Ascertain what muscles are weak, what portion of the body is most in need of exercise; then practice such as will bring about the desired result. Strength and symmetrical development are sure to ensue.

No. 1. The fore-arm.
No. 2. The extreme upper arm.
No. 3. The upper chest.
No. 4. The entire chest.
No. 5. The extreme point of the shoulder.
No. 6. The front and back of the upper arm (biceps and triceps).
No. 7. The shoulder.
No. 8. The shoulder, and the side of the chest.
No. 9-10-11. The abdomen, the small of the back, and the sides.
No. 12. The extreme upper part of the shoulder.
No. 13. The lower thigh—inner, front and back.
No. 14. The entire calf, the thigh, the ankle and the foot.
No. 14-19. The neck—as per 14 to 19 in *exercises without apparatus*.
No. 15. The thigh—front, back, and the extreme upper inner portion.

No. 16. The thigh—the lower front and the lower back.

No. 17. The thigh—the inner portion.

Note.—It will be observed that we have studiously avoided the use of technical terms.

The Indian club exercises are intended to strengthen and invigorate the entire body, but their use is especially designed to develop the muscles of the waist, chest, arms and shoulders.

The exercises without the use of apparatus, will give freedom and flexibility to the joints, at the same time strengthening and developing many of the muscles.

The dumb-bells will, when adhering to the system herein given, bring into action *all* the muscles, thus producing a *symmetrical* development of the body.

While we advocate (and take) *all* the exercises, we especially commend—as a morning tonic—Exercise No. 25 (without apparatus), and Exercise No. 28—with the two clubs.

WARMAN'S DUMB-BELL EXERCISES.

Should these exercises be given *without* dumb-bells, keep the hands closed. Characterize each movement by a strong, vigorous action.

The expense of the dumb-bells, however, is so trifling, the space they occupy of so little moment, the results derived therefrom so beneficial, that the author recommends their use.

There is nothing to be gained by *heavy* dumb-bell work. Yet the exercises here given should not be classed under *light* calisthenics. While the *dumb-bell* that is used should be *light*, the *force* whereby it is used should be *heavy*.

Knowing that wooden dumb-bells—even those of the same weight—have not always the same sized handle, and that the majority of the handles are too small for the average sized hand, we have arranged, in consequence of this difficulty, with Messrs. Spalding & Bros., of Chicago and New York, to make for us what is known as

WARMAN'S DUMB-BELL SUBSTITUTE.

These substitutes have given perfect satisfaction; are more durable than the wooden dumb-bell; are highly polished, with an ebony finish; will not mar by striking them together; will serve alike for the smallest or the largest hand; will occupy but very little space; can be carried in the pocket; and last, but not the least to be considered, they are *less expensive* than the wooden dumb-bells.

GENERAL DIRECTIONS.

Music. — Portions of army selections, such as "*Tramp, tramp, tramp,*" and "*Marching through Georgia,*" are especially adaptable for class work.

Grasp the dumb-bells firmly, and cause every movement to be one of vigorous action.

The number of moves in each exercise should correspond with the impulses of the music—the number of impulses being optional with the teacher.

We would suggest as a criterion, that, in taking the first exercise to the tune of "Tramp, tramp, tramp," etc., the change to the second exercise should occur directly after the seventh upward impulse. In taking the second exercise, the change occurs directly after the seventh impulse to the right.

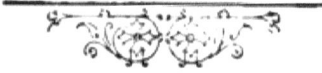

EXERCISE 1.

Extend the arms to the side, as shown in the illustration. Do this when position is called or the signal given by the music.

The hands should rise and fall with each musical impulse. Bring the hands down and in under as far as possible, and then up as far as possible. Do not move the arms except at the wrist joint.

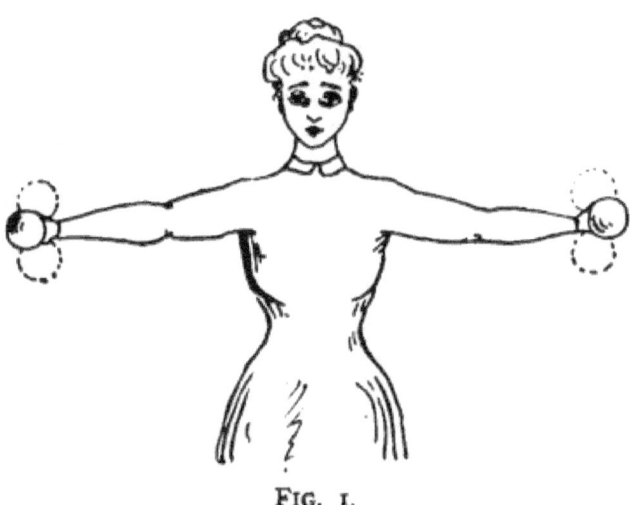

FIG. 1.

Position. Down—Up—Down—Up.
             ''   ''   ''   ''
             ''   ''   ''
             ''   ''   change.

EXERCISE 2.

At the conclusion of the seventh upward impulse of Exercise 1, keep the arms extended, but turn or twist the arm to the right, then to the left. This movement will affect the whole arm and the shoulder. Do not lower the arm, but keep it extended during the exercise. Do not loosen the grasp on the bells.

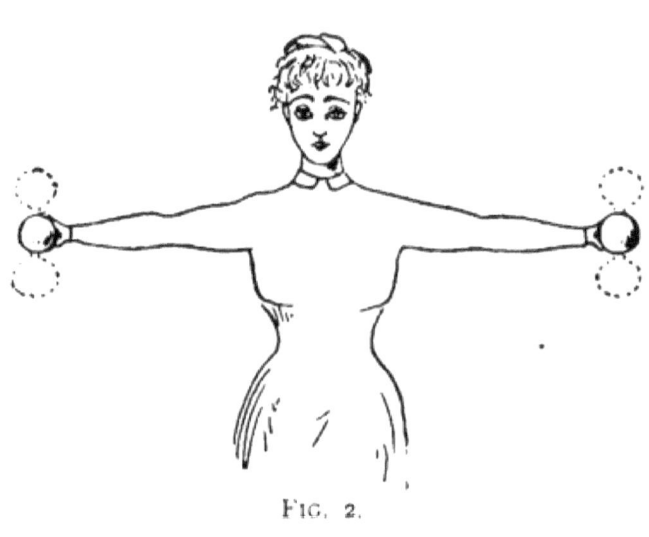

Fig. 2.

Turn. Right—Left—Right—Left.
  "   "   "   "   "
  "   "   "   "   "
  "   change.

EXERCISE 3.

Bring the arms forward on a direct line, as shown in the illustration. Strike the bells together, and return them on the same line, carrying them just a little back of position. Do not *lower* the arms nor bend the body in the foolish endeavor to try to strike the back of the hands behind you. If the hands are kept on a direct line with the shoulder, and the body kept erect, not one person in ten thousand can strike the back of the hands together. When the bells pass back, do not *bend* the body, but allow it to sway.

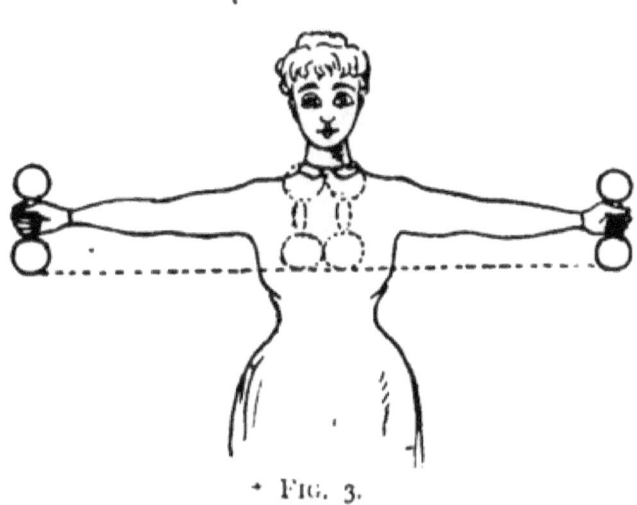

Fig. 3.

Front—Back—Front—Back.
 "   "   "   "
 "   "   "   "
 "   change at will.

EXERCISE 4.

Make the change from the front position of the last exercise, bringing the hands back to the side, as shown in the illustration. Place the bells vertically against the ribs, but *do not bend the wrist.* Thrust the arms forward and back. Bring the hands back to the ribs each time—with *unbent* wrist.

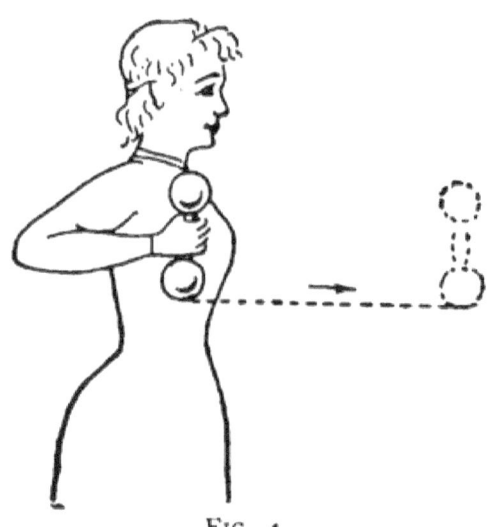

FIG. 4.

Back—Front—Back—Front.
 "   "   "   "
 "   "   "   "
 "   Change at will.

EXERCISE 5.

When the hands are drawn back the last time in the preceding exercise, thrust them down with force; then bring them up under the arms to the armpits. Bend the wrists as much as possible, when the hands touch the armpits, but bring the arm up perfectly straight, as shown in the illustration.

In throwing the arms down with force, remove the weight of the body from the heel. By so doing the jarring of the body will be avoided, as well as the jarring of the room, and possibly the jarring of some one's nerves. Do not *bend* the body, but incline it forward.

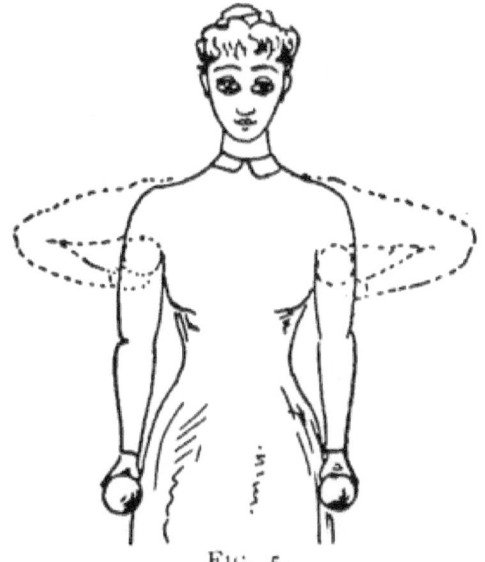

FIG. 5.

Down—Up—Down—Up.
 ,,   ,,   ,,   ,,
 ,,   ,,   ,,   ,,

Change at will

EXERCISE 6.

On the last upward move, thrust the arms out at the side, with the hands on a line with the shoulders. Thrust out and back with force, taking care not to lower the elbows, and not to bend the wrists. See illustration. The bell should not strike the shoulder.

Fig. 6.

Out—Back—Out—Back.

Change at will.

EXERCISE 7.

Thrust the hands up, as shown in the illustration. The bells may be allowed to click, if thought desirable. In bringing the bells down, touch the shoulders with them without lowering the arm. Make an effort to extend the arms as far as possible above the head.

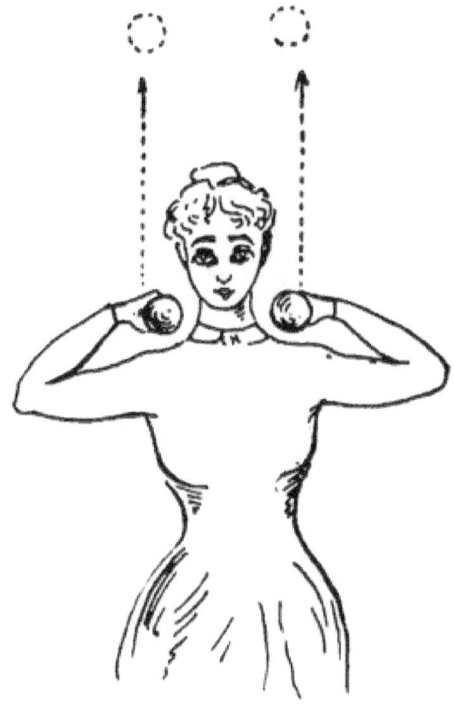

FIG. 7.

Up—Down—Up—Down.

Change at will.

EXERCISE 8.

Place the left hand at the side—the arm akimbo, the hand resting against the ribs. Extend the right arm forward, as shown in the illustration. Sweep the hand toward the floor, making a complete and perfect circle at the right side.

We would suggest the making of about three full circles forward, and three full circles reversed. Then bring the *right* hand to the side—the arm akimbo—and extend the *left* arm forward for three full sweeps forward and toward the floor, and the three reverse movements.

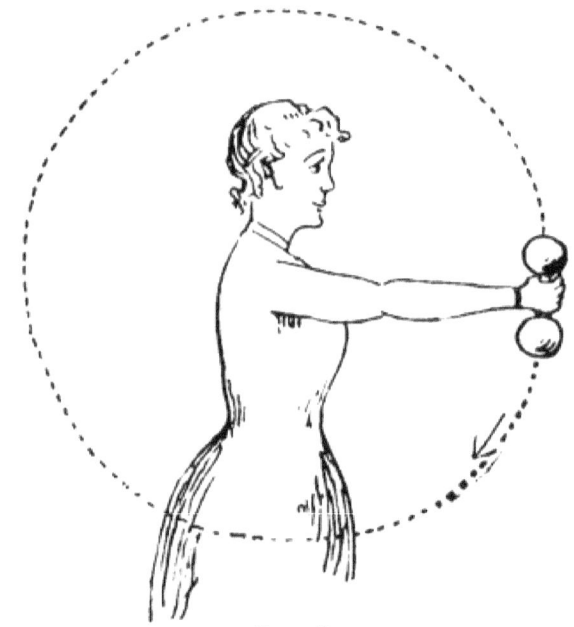

FIG. 8.

Right.	Forward and sweep.		1-2-3.
	Reverse "	"	1-2-3.
Left.	Forward "	"	1-2-3.
	Reverse "		1-2-3.

EXERCISE 9.

Return the left hand to the side; both arms will then be akimbo. Change the music to very slow march time. The arms will now rest while the waist muscles are being exercised.

Bend the body *slowly* forward and as far down as possible, then up and as far back and down as possible, bending the knees on the backward movement. Do not allow any jerkiness in this and the next two exercises, but instead, a feeling akin to the stretching of the body—especially of the muscles of the back and abdomen.

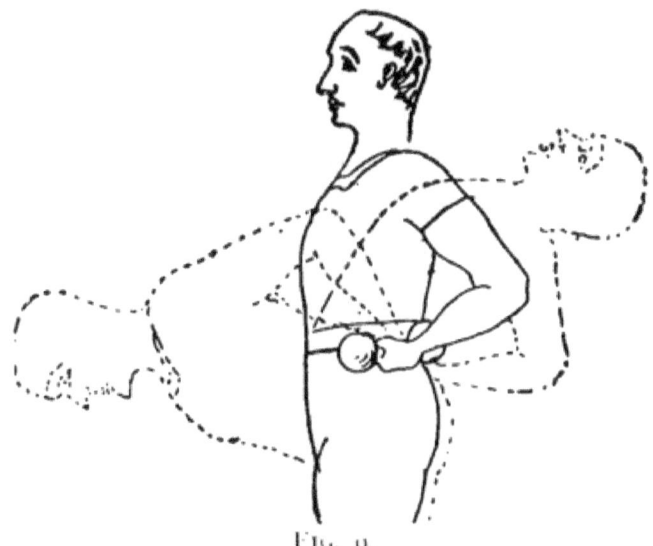

Fig. 9.

Forward—Up—Backward—Up.
"   "   "   "
"   "   "   "

Change at will.

EXERCISE 10.

Bend the body to the right as far as possible, then up and to the left as far as possible, *without raising either foot from the floor*. Keep the bells at the side—arms akimbo. There should be strong tension of the muscles on either side. Make the movements very slowly.

Fig. 10.

Right—Up—Left—Up.

Change at will.

EXERCISE 11.

Twist or turn the body as far as possible to the right, then to the left. Do not move the feet, or bend the body forward or backward, or from side to side Make the movements very slowly.

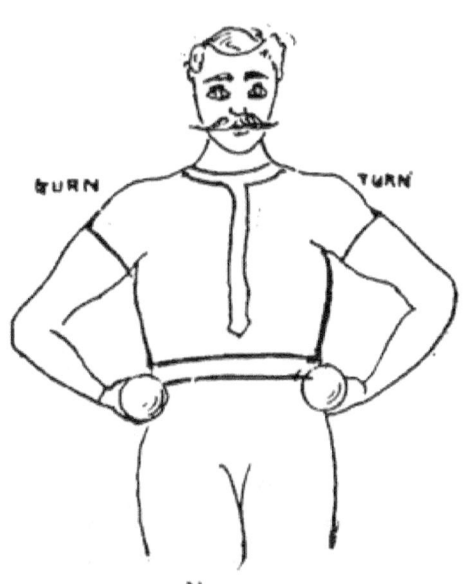

Fig. 11.

Right—Left—Right—Left.
   "   "   "   "
   "   "   "   "

Change at will.

EXERCISE 12.

Drop the hands down so that the arms are pendant at the side. Turn the palms outward, with the back of the hands touching the limbs. Extend the arms outward and up, as shown in the illustration. Keep the arms as straight as possible, touching the bells together as far above the head as possible, without moving the feet. Bring the bells back to the side of the body with the arms still extended. Each time that the bells are brought down, touch the limbs with the back of the hands.

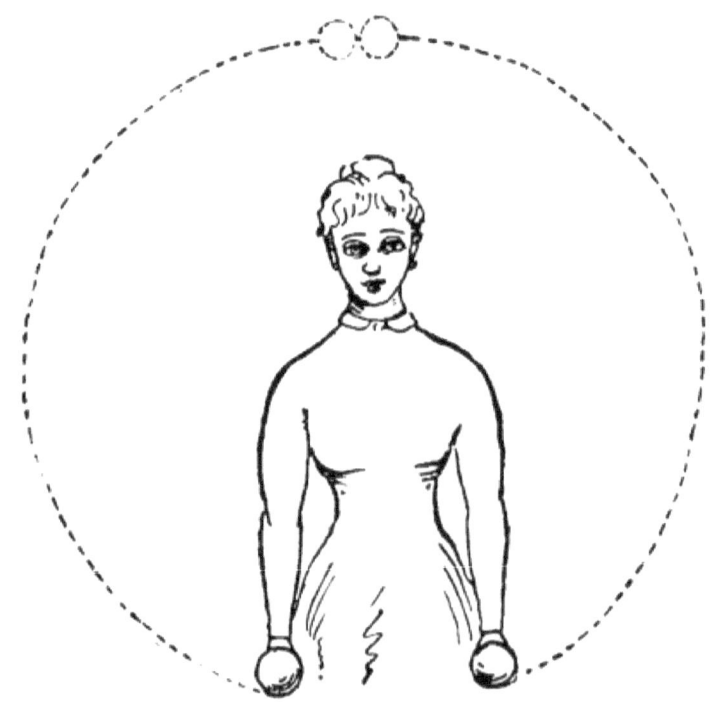

FIG. 12.

Turn. Up—Down—Up—Down.
    " " " "
    " " " "

Change at will.

EXERCISE 13.

Bring the hands to the side with the bells vertical, as shown in the illustration. Keep the left hand in position during the movement of the right, and *vice versa*. Step well forward, as shown in the illustration. Bend the right knee, and place the right hand to the floor by the side of the right foot. Turn the left foot on the side and keep the limb unbent. Spring back to position. Take the same exercise with the left limb, placing **the left hand on the floor by the side of the left foot.**

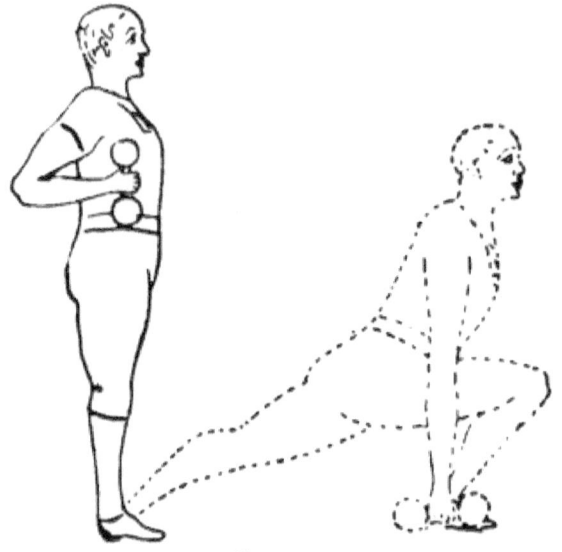

FIG. 13.

Right.   Forward—Up—Forward—Up.

Left.

Change at will.

EXERCISE 14.

Place the hands upon the side, as shown in the illustration. Stand erect. Rise slowly on the toes, raising the heels as far as possible from the floor. Poise a few seconds, then allow the heels to touch the floor, but do not sink heavily upon them, nor allow the body to sway backward and forward.

Fig. 14.

Up—Down—Up—Down.

From 10 to 50 times.

EXERCISE 15.

Place the right hand to the left chest, as shown in the illustration. Step quite a distance to the right, on a straight line with the left foot. Do not take up the left foot from the floor, but turn it on the side, with the limb unbent. Swing the right hand down and up till the bell hangs over the right shoulder. Pass back to position, sweeping the bell back to the chest.

The same exercise should be taken to the left side.

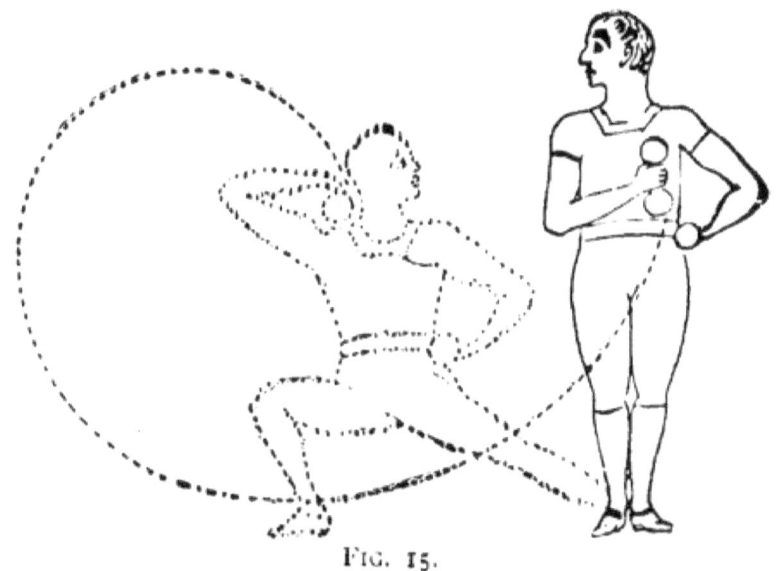

FIG. 15.

Right—Place—Sweep—Position.
     " "
     " "
Left—Place " "
     " "
     " "

EXERCISE 16.

Place the hands on the chest. Thrust them straight up, then back to the chest, then to the floor, as shown in the illustration. Touch the bells to the floor by the side of the feet. Keep the body erect from the waist up. Pass up to position, bringing the bells again to the chest.

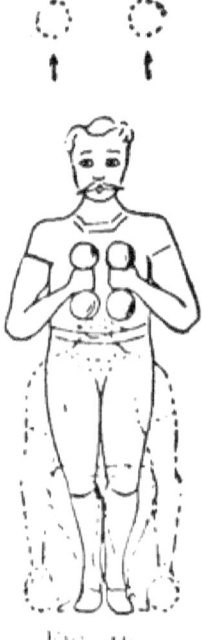

Fig. 16.

Chest—Up—Chest—Floor.
" " " "
" " " "

Change at will.

EXERCISE 17.

Place the arms as shown in the illustration. Make a sweep to the floor, placing the bells by the side of the feet, and leaving them there, while sweeping the hands far enough back to complete a three-fourths circle from first position. Straighten the limbs, but not the body, when sweeping the hands back.

On the return movement bend the limbs, take the bells from the floor, and sweep them up and back of the head to position.

FIG. 17.

Position. Sweep—Floor—Halt. Return—Take—Up.
"   "   "   "   "   "   "
"   "   "   "   "   "   "

Conclude the exercises by placing the hands to the chest, and filing right or left, and marching.

WARMAN'S INDIAN-CLUB SYSTEM.
ONE CLUB.

GENERAL DIRECTIONS.

Grasp the club firmly, but easily; the little finger resting against the knob. As these exercises are intended for physical development, and not for the purpose of displaying "fancy" or "snake movements" —very good in their way and for the purpose designed —it is advisable and necessary that the knob of the club should never slip to the thumb and forefinger; neither should the thumb extend up the handle of the club. Place the idle arm at the side, with the back of the fingers resting gracefully against the side of the body. Do not allow the club to wabble. When a movement is made requiring the arm to be extended, hold the club firmly, yet as gracefully as if it were a part of that extension. Imagine that you are standing between perfect circles at right angles with each other—large and small on either side; large in front and small behind. The clubs should follow these lines perfectly in all the small circles and sweeps.

Be satisfied to practice with one club till all the single moves have been mastered; the double moves will then be more readily attained, as they are combinations of the single.

Practice each move separately, as shown in the illustration of the same. Learn the *name* of each move, and it will be helpful, inasmuch as it is suggestive.

Do not be ambitious to handle heavy clubs. Judicious practice regularly taken with a pair of *light* clubs, will prove more beneficial than spasmodic or overwork with *heavy* clubs. Stand firmly, but not rigidly. Place the feet in as graceful and comfortable a position as the nature of the movement will allow. Do not quite touch the heels, nor place them too far apart, when facing an audience.

SIZE OF CLUBS.

We have observed that, as a general thing, a lady of average strength will use a two-pound club with ease; a gentleman, a four-pound club. These are sufficiently heavy for beginners, especially when taking our entire system of exercises without rest, giving each movement three times.

ERRATA.
INDIAN-CLUB SYSTEM.
ONE CLUB.

Figures 15 to 22 inclusive should face to the left—as directed in the instructions accompanying the illustrations.

WARMAN'S INDIAN-CLUB SYSTEM.
ONE CLUB.

POSITION.

Place the club in the hands, as shown in POSITION. Toss the club a little higher than the head, placing the left hand against the side of the body, the back of the fingers touching the body. Pass the right hand back of the head at the right side, and allow the club to drop and form a complete small circle back of the head, which we will designate as the *small inward*. Follow this movement with a full sweep of the arm in front toward the left side, bringing it up on the right to make *two* small inwards, etc., thus forming Fig. 1.

FIG. 1.

INWARD—RIGHT.

1 Small circle inward - Sweep in front.
2   "   "   "   -   "   "   "
3   "   "   "   -   "   "   "

CHANGE—by halting the club, just as it sweeps up the right side, a little higher than the shoulder—and reverse the movement.

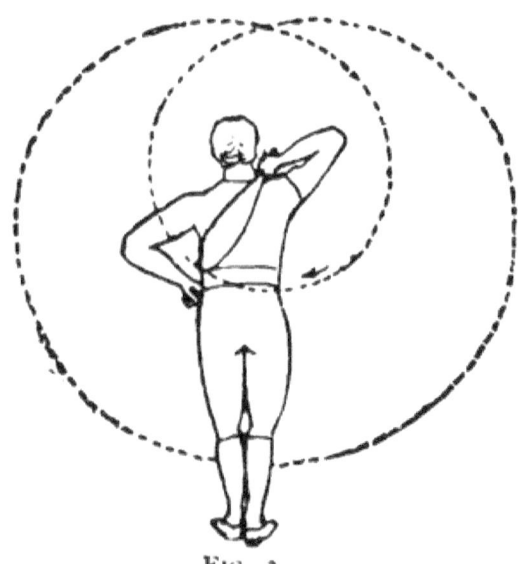

FIG. 2.

OUTWARD—RIGHT.

1 Small circle outward—Sweep in front.
2 "   "   "   "   "   "
3 "   "   "   "   "   "

CHANGE.—by passing the club to the left hand just as it sweeps up toward the left side the third time. When a little higher than the shoulder, let it fall to a small outward circle.

FIG. 3.

OUTWARD—LEFT.

1 Small circle outward—sweep in front.
2 " " " " " "
3 " " " " " "

CHANGE—by omitting the third sweep outward, but instead, drop the club in front of the face, following with a full sweep inward, bringing up the club on the left side and making a small inward circle.

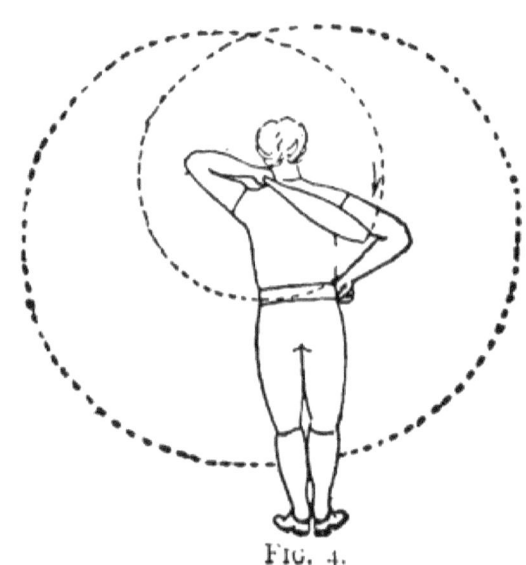

FIG. 4.

INWARD—LIFT.

1 Small circle inward—Sweep in front.
2 "   "   "   "   "   "
3 "   "   "   "

CHANGE—by halting the club when it sweeps up the left side the third time, poising it as shown in the illustration. Let it fall as if to make an outward, but instead of making a full circle, drop it in front of the face.

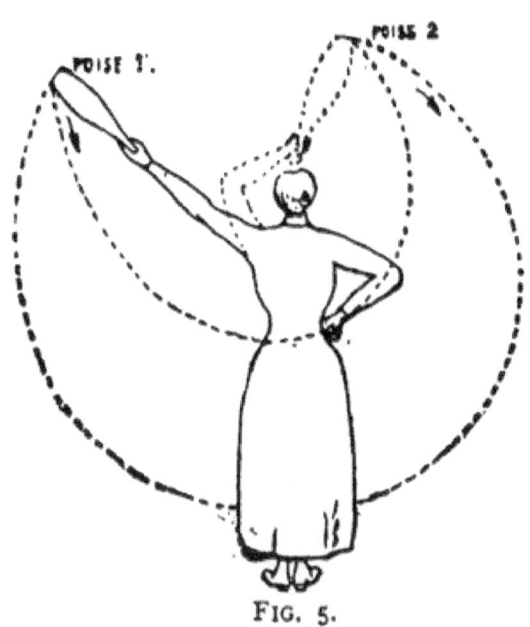

FIG. 5.

POISE—DROP. LEFT.

Poise at 1—Poise at 2—Drop in front of the face.
"   "   "   "   "   "   "   "
"   "   "   "   "   "   "   "

CHANGE—by poising again at 1, reversing the movement to a small outward; then sweep it in front, taking it up with the right hand and halting it at poise 1 on the right side. Let it fall as if to make an outward; but instead of making a full circle, drop it in front of the face.

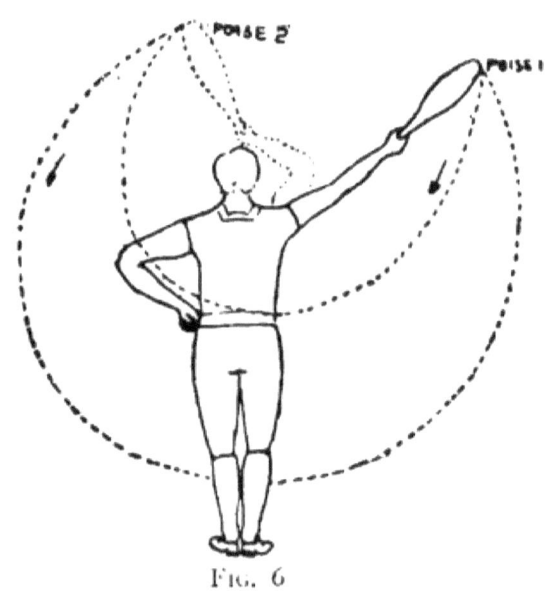

Fig. 6

POISE—DROP. RIGHT.

Poise at 1—Poise at 2—Drop in front of the face.
" "   " "   "   "   "   "   "   "
" "   " "   "   "   "   "   "   "

CHANGE—by poising again at 1, and reversing the movement to a small outward; then sweep it in front and take it up with the left hand to poise 1 left; reverse it to a small outward, and pass it from hand to hand after each small outward.

FIG. 7.

ALTERNATING OUTWARD.

Outward—Right—Sweep. Outward—Left—Sweep.

CHANGE—by taking the club again in the right hand as if to make a fourth outward, but instead, make a small inward, passing it quickly behind the head to the left hand, which should be in position to grasp the club without stopping its motion. It will drop into a small outward circle with the left hand. Sweep it out and front, pass it again to the right hand.

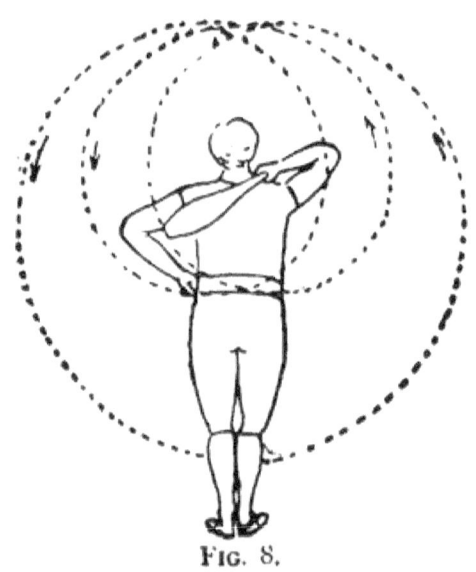

FIG. 8.

LARGE WHEEL—LEFT.

Inward—Right—Outward—Left—Sweep.
"   "   "   "   "
"   "   "   "   Drop.

132   PHYSICAL TRAINING.

CHANGE—by omitting the last sweep, but, instead, drop the club in front of the face with the left hand, giving a full sweep inward, thus reversing the movement.

FIG. 9.

LARGE WHEEL—RIGHT.

Inward—Left.	Outward—Right.	Sweep.
"	"	"
"	"	"
"	"	Drop.

CHANGE—by again omitting the last sweep. Drop the club in front of the face with the right hand, giving a full sweep inward, thus reversing the movement.

FIG. 10.

SMALL WHEEL—LEFT.

Inward—Right. Outward—Left. Avoid Sweep.
"   "   "   "
"   "   "   Drop.

CHANGE—by dropping the club in front of the face with the left hand, following with a full sweep inward, thus reversing the movement.

It will be observed that, in making the small wheels, the sweeps are omitted, thus distinguishing between the large and small wheels.

FIG. II.

SMALL WHEEL.—RIGHT.

Inward—Left.	Outward—Right.	Avoid Sweep.
" "	" "	" "
" "	" "	Drop and Poise.

CHANGE—by again dropping the club in front of the face with the right, giving a full sweep inward; but, as the club comes up, halt it at poise 1, swing it to poise 2, and drop in front of the face, bringing it to an inward. Sweep it in front and halt it again at poise 1.

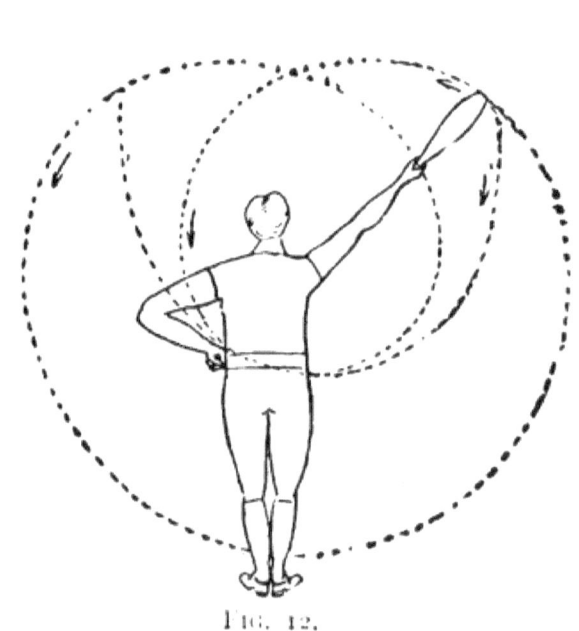

FIG. 12.

POISE—DROP—INWARD. RIGHT.

Poise at 1—Poise at 2—Drop—Inward—Sweep.

Pass Over.

CHANGE—by passing the club to the left hand, making the change back of the head. Pass from the last small inward circle with the right hand to a small outward with the left. Drop the club in front of the face and sweep it up to poise 1, swing it to poise 2, and then drop it in front of the face, and bring it to an inward. Sweep it in front, and halt it again at poise 1.

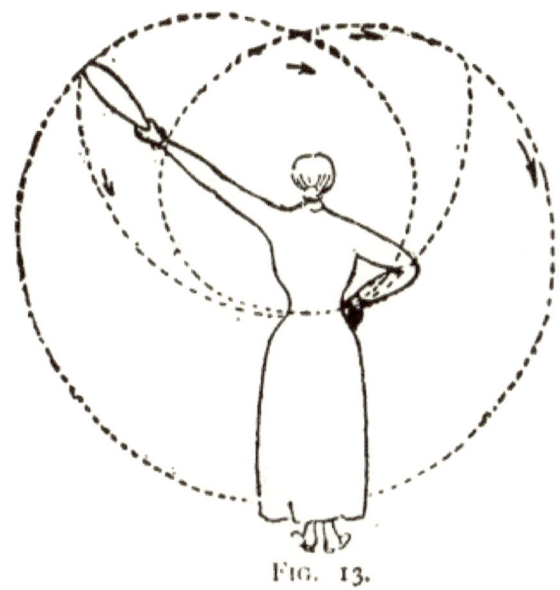

FIG. 13.

POISE—DROP—INWARD. LIFT.

Poise at 1—Poise at 2—Drop Inward—Sweep.
" " " " " " " " " "
" " " " " " " " " Pass Over.

CHANGE—by passing the club to the right hand, making the change back of the head, going from a small inward left to a small outward right. Drop the club in front of the face and sweep it to an inward right, passing it directly back to the left hand—making the change back of the head—and making a drop and inward left.

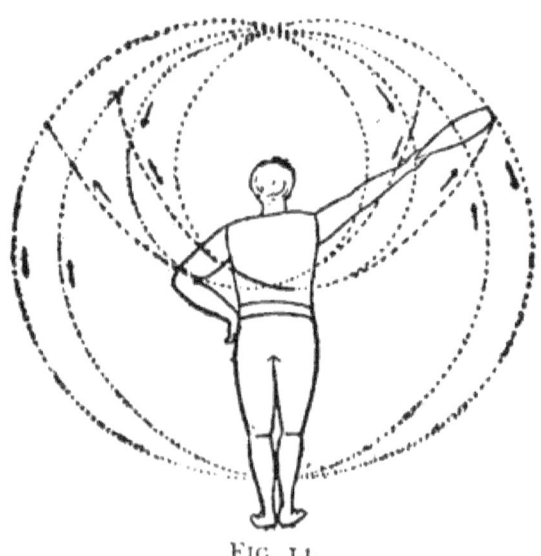

FIG. 14.

ALTERNATING DROP AND INWARD.

Drop—Sweep—Inward—Over.   Drop—Sweep—Inward—Over.
"   "   "   "   "   "   "   "
"   "   "   Turn the body to the left.

138   PHYSICAL TRAINING.

CHANGE—by turning the body to the left just as the club is completing the last small inward circle. Keep the arm bent, and make a wrist circle at the side. Keep a firm hold on the club, not allowing the knob to slip to the thumb and fore finger.

FIG. 15.

SMALL SIDE.

Small side-circle.   1-2-3.

CHANGE—by extending the arm upward and forward, making a large circle at the side without bending the arm.

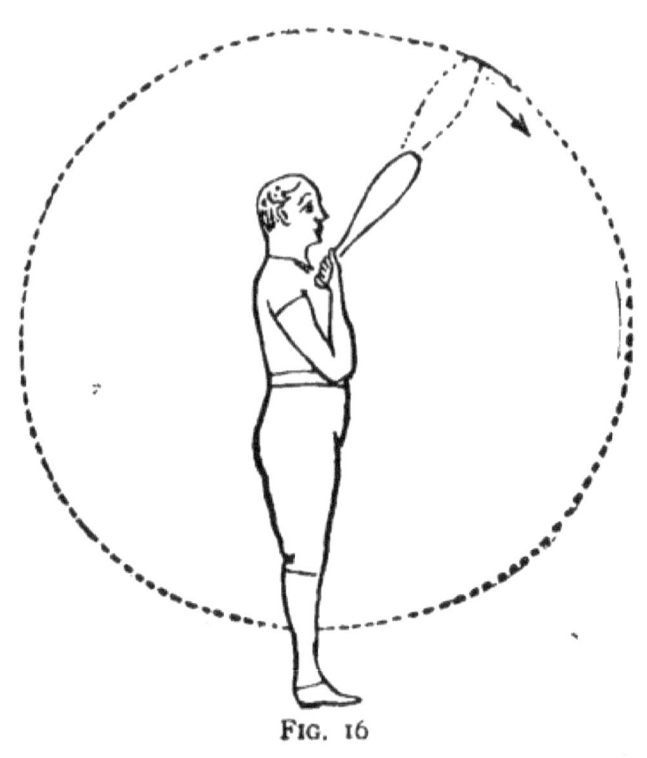

FIG. 16

LARGE SIDE.

Large side-circles. 1-2-3.

140   PHYSICAL TRAINING.

CHANGE—by checking the club just as it passes the feet on the third downward stroke, and reversing the movement. Do not allow the club to wabble when checking it, nor the arm to bend in making the circle.

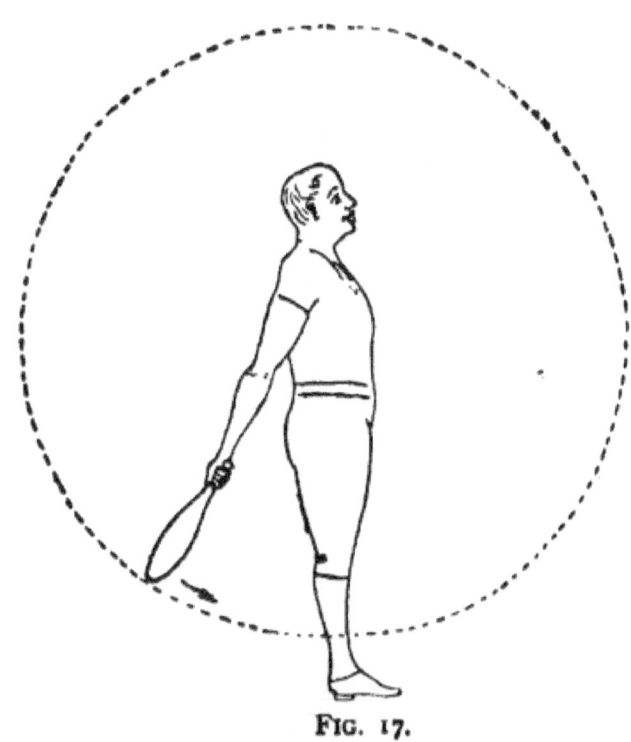

FIG. 17.

REVERSE.
Large side Reverse. 1—2—3.

CHANGE—as the club comes up in front on the third circle. When it is high enough, drop it to a *small* side, followed by a *large* side; then, as it is ready to descend as if to make a *second* large side, bring it diagonally to the left side with a full sweep; then back to the starting point of a large side, and *make* another large side-circle.

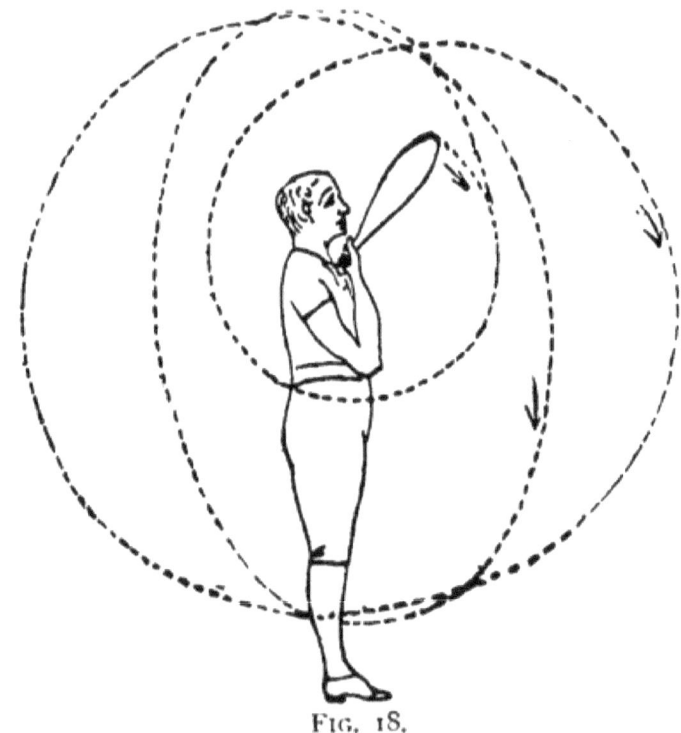

FIG. 18.

SIDE AND DIAGONAL.

1 Small—Large—Diagonal—Large.
2 " " " "
3 " and over.

CHANGE.—at the close of the third small circle, by making a small inward and passing the club to the left hand, making the change back of the head. Make a small outward with the left, and when the club becomes vertical, drop it back to a small inward with the same hand, and when the club again becomes vertical, change the movement to a small side-circle.

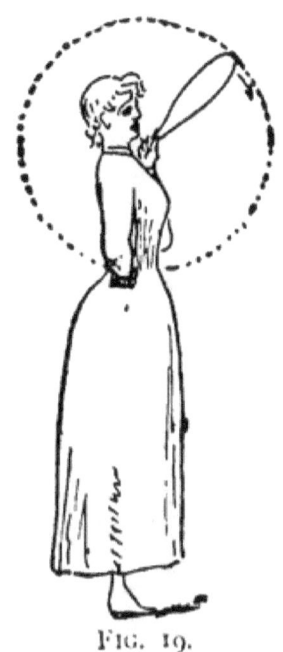

FIG. 19.

SMALL SIDE.

Small side-circle.   1-2-3.

CHANGE—by extending the arm upward and forward, making a *large* circle at the side, without bending the arm.

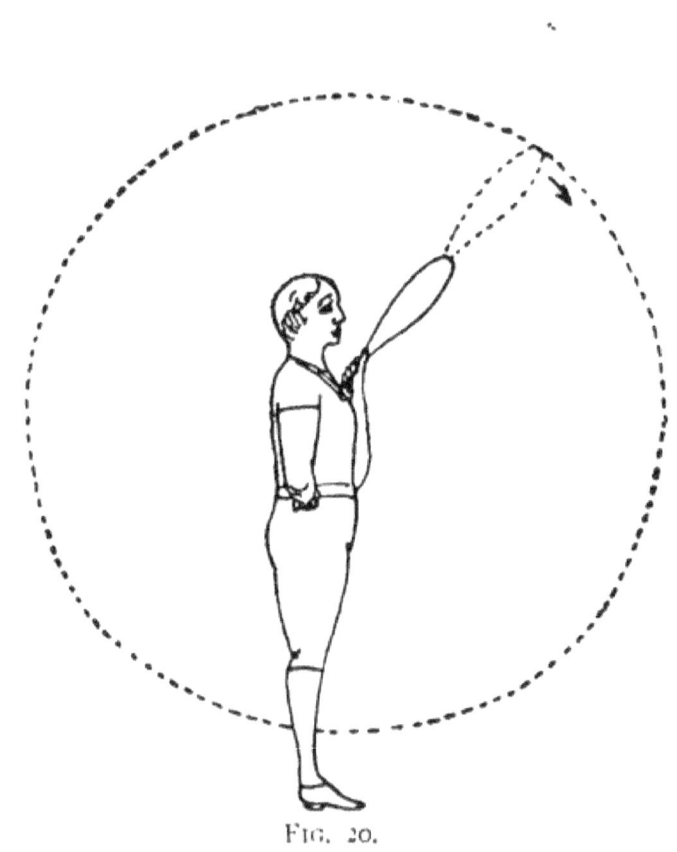

FIG. 20.

LARGE SIDE.
Large side circle—1-2-3.

CHANGE—by checking the club just as it passes the feet on the third downward stroke, and reversing the movement. Do not allow the club to wabble when checking it, nor the arm to bend, when making the circle.

FIG. 21.

REVERSE.

Large side—Reverse.   1-2-3.

CHANGE—as the club comes up in front on the third circle. When it is high enough, drop it to a *small* side, followed by a *large* side; then, as it is ready to descend as if to make a *second* large side, bring it diagonally to the right side with a full sweep; then back to the starting point of a large side, and *make* another large side-circle.

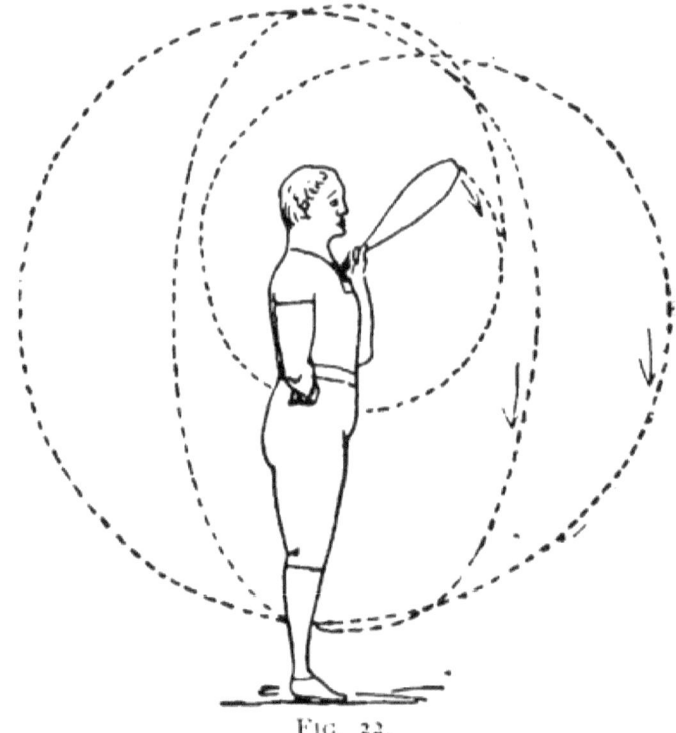

FIG. 22.

SIDE AND DIAGONAL.

1 Small—Large—Diagonal—Large.
2 "   "   "   "
3 " and face front.

CHANGE—by extending the arm at the completion of the third small circle, as if to make a large side circle; then, just as the club is ready to sweep down, turn the body quickly back to the front position. Sweep the club in front, make a small outward with the left hand, and sweep it to the right. Place the right hand as shown in the illustration, and make small circles outside and inside the arm, keeping the arm extended as much as possible, and keep the club as *near* the arm as possible. *Keep the little finger next to the knob.*

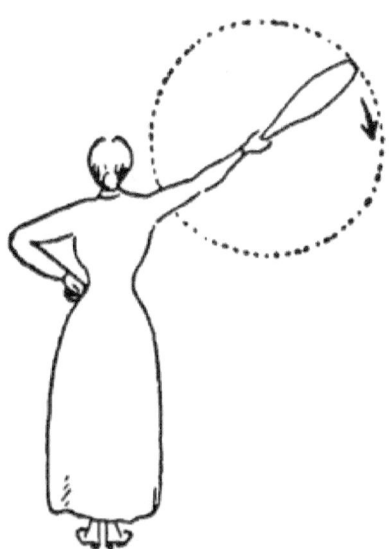

FIG. 23.

CHIN-KNOCKER.

Outside of arm—Inside of arm.
"   "   "   "   "   "
"   "   "   "   "   "
"   "   "   Sweep to the left hand.

CHANGE.—by sweeping the club to the left hand and making a small outward with the left. Place the hand, as shown in the illustration, and make small circles outside and inside the arm, keeping the arm extended as much as possible; also keep the club moving as *near* the arm as possible. Do not let the knob of the club slip to the thumb and forefinger.

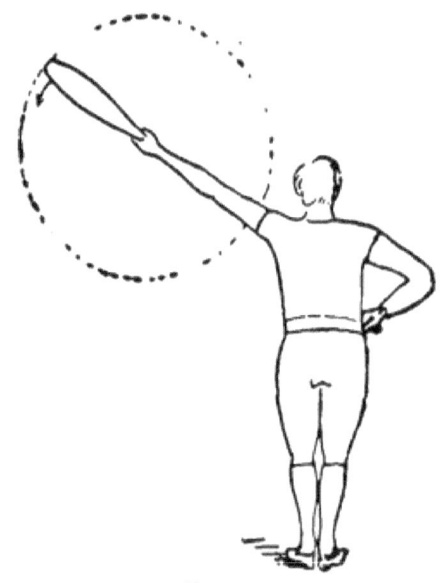

FIG. 24.

CHIN-KNOCKER.

Outside of arm—Inside of arm.
" " " " " "
" " " " " "
" " " Sweep to the right hand.

CHANGE.—by carrying the club to the right side by the right hand, until the hand is straight with the shoulder, as seen in the illustration. Grasp the club firmly, and hold it in an upright position. Without *raising, lowering* or *bending* the arm the *slightest*, lay the club on the arm, then raise it and extend it till it is perfectly straight. Throughout this entire exercise the arm should not move, nor bend at the elbow.

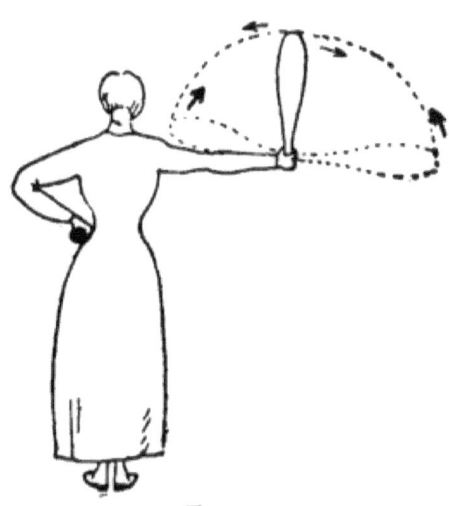

FIG. 25.

THE LEVER.

Upright—On the arm—Straight out.
" " " " "
" " " " "
" " " and toss to outward.

CHANGE—by tossing the club to a small outward, and sweep it to the left hand; stop the hand as soon as it is even with the shoulder, and place the club in an upright position. Lay the club on the arm without bending the arm at the elbow. Raise the club without moving the arm, and extend it until it is perfectly straight, as shown in the illustration.

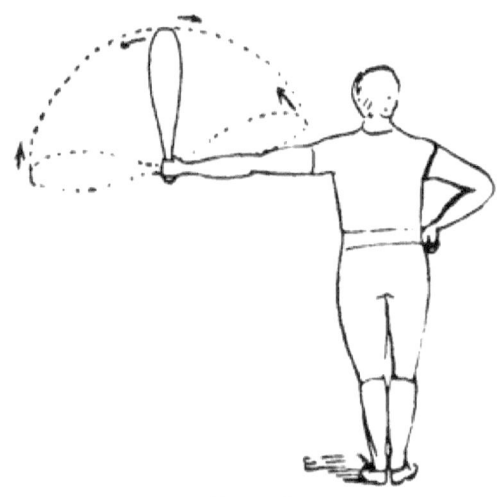

FIG. 26.

THE LEVER.

Upright—On the arm—Straight out.
.. ..
.. ..
.. .. and toss to outward.

CHANGE—by tossing the club to a small outward. Do not make a sweep, but just as the club completes the small circle, reverse it to a small inward. Then, just as the club is upright, make a small side-circle, and when the club is again upright, make a small inward; thus alternating small inwards and small sides.

FIG. 27.

INWARD AND SIDE.

Small inward—Small side.
" " " "
" " " "
" " and over to the right.

CHANGE—by passing the club back of the head to the right hand. Make a small outward with the right hand, then reverse it to a small inward, and, as it comes to an upright position, change it to a small side circle, then back to a small inward; thus alternating small sides and small inwards

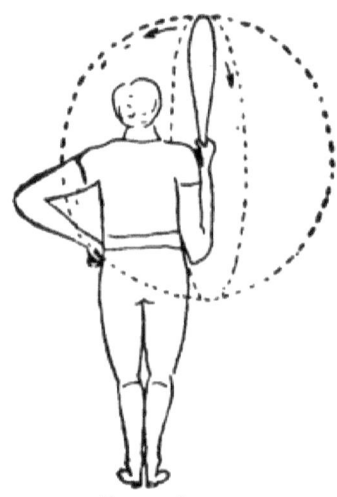

FIG. 28.

INWARD AND SIDE.

Small inward—Small side.
" " " "
" " " "
" " and toss over the head, letting it drop gently in the left hand, as shown in Fig. 1—position. This will give a graceful

FINISH.

WARMAN'S INDIAN-CLUB SYSTEM.
CONDENSED FOR CALLING.—ONE CLUB.

Pre-supposing that the pupil has become familiar with all the movements; *i. e.*, with the necessary *details* in the learning of each, we present herewith our system of exercises in a *condensed* form, as a reminder to the individual, or as an aid to the teacher in calling the movements to a class

The order of exercises, and the number of movements of each, are the same as we use for our classes in their public exhibitions.

On the rostrum, at the close of our lecture on "PHYSICAL TRAINING, or THE CARE OF THE BODY," we aim not only to entertain, but to exemplify the principles set forth in our lecture, by giving, in appropriate costume, our entire system of Indian-Club exercises—our clubs weighing eight pounds each.

As a rule, we do not advocate the use of heavy clubs; but these to us do not seem heavy, having had them in use—privately and publicly—for twenty-one years.

Our plan of work is on the principle of the HEALTH LIFT; *i. e.*: "cumulative strength"—the only *true* principle. Hence we advise the use of one club throughout the entire system of exercises; then rest a moment before swinging the two clubs. Rest again, if desirable, at the close of "the windmill," before concluding the entire system.

By so doing we find no difficulty in closing our evening's entertainment by a few movements with *both clubs* (16 lbs.) *in one hand.*

By adhering to these suggestions, *invigoration* will take the place of *exhaustion*. Be patient in well doing.

ONE CLUB.

No. 1. Inward Right—one.
" " two.
" " three.
No. 2. Outward Right—one.
" " two.
" " three.
No. 3. Outward Left—one.
" " two.
" " three. Drop.
No. 4. Inward Left—one.
" " two.
" " three.
No. 5. Poise and Drop—Left. 1-2-3.
No. 6. Poise and Drop—Right. 1-2-3.
No. 7. Outward Right—Outward Left.
" " " "
" " " "
No. 8. Large Wheel—Left. 1-2-3. Drop and reverse.
No. 9. Large Wheel—Right. 1-2-3. Drop and reverse.
No. 10. Small Wheel—Left. 1-2-3. Drop and reverse.
No. 11. Small Wheel—Right. 1-2-3. Drop and Poise.
No. 12. Poise—Drop—Inward—Right. 1-2-3. Over.
No. 13. Poise—Drop—Inward—Left. 1-2-3. Over.
No. 14. Drop—Inward—Right—Over.
Drop—Inward—Left—Over.
Drop—Inward—Right—Over.
Drop—Inward—Left—Over
Drop—Inward—Right—Turn.

No. 15. Small Side—Right.   1-2-3.
No. 16. Large Side—Right.   1-2-3.
No. 17. Reverse—Right.   1-2-3.
No. 18. Small—Large—Diagonal—Large.
   2 "   "   "   "
   3 "   Change to left hand.
No. 19. Small Side—Left.   1-2-3.
No. 20. Large Side—Left.   1-2-3.
No. 21. Reverse—Left.   1-2-3.
No. 22. Small—Large—Diagonal—Large.
   2 "   "   "   "
   3 "   Turn.   Change to right.
No. 23. Chin-knocker—Right.   1-2-3.
No. 24. Chin knocker—Left.   1-2-3.
No. 25. Lever—Right.   1-2-3.
No. 26. Lever—Left.   1-2-3.
No. 27. Inward and Small Side—Left.   1-2-3.
No. 28. Inward and Small Side—Right.   1-2-3.

Finish by tossing the club over the head, dropping it gently into the left hand.

WARMAN'S INDIAN-CLUB SYSTEM.
TWO CLUBS.

GENERAL DIRECTIONS.

When the clubs fall in the same direction, and are intended to drop simultaneously, they should not be separated from each other any greater distance *during* the movement than when the movement *began*.

With the single exception of a "follow" movement (The windmill, Fig. 12) both clubs should drop with the same impulse, even though they are making different movements. The slightest variation from this rule will destroy the gracefulness and beauty of the swinging.

When facing front, avoid turning the body from side to side, except in Fig. 1. Practice before a mirror in order that every movement of the club may be seen while facing front. This will teach one to look at his audience, instead of turning his head and watching the clubs. Master your clubs instead of allowing them to master you.

ERRATA.
INDIAN-CLUB SYSTEM.
TWO CLUBS.

Fig. 24 should face to the left—as directed in the instruction accompanying the illustration.

WARMAN'S INDIAN-CLUB SYSTEM.
TWO CLUBS.

Take position by pointing the two clubs to the left, as shown in the illustration. Keep the palms of the hands up in order to steady the clubs. Toss both clubs up and out, sweeping them down in front of the body, and bringing them up to left side. Avoid angles. Toss them out and bring them in as if describing an arc of a circle.

N. B.—To take up the clubs artistically—which cannot be done until all the movements shall have been learned—see page 187.

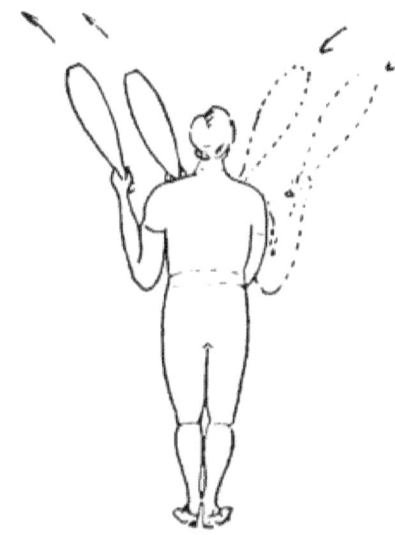

Fig. 1.

POINT.

Point left—Sweep   Point right—Sweep.
"   "   "   "   "   "
"   "   "   "   "   "
"   " Halt.

PHYSICAL TRAINING. 157

CHANGE—by halting at position and making a small outward with the left, and a full sweep with the right; both clubs dropping simultaneously. The club in the right hand makes a large revolution, while the one in the left makes a small one.

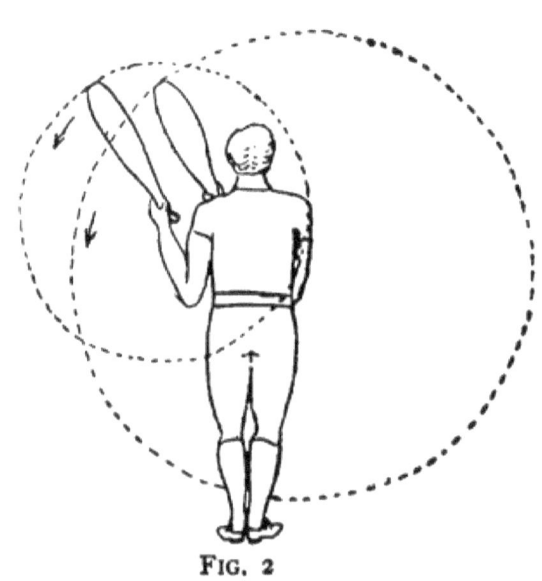

FIG. 2

SMALL LEFT—LARGE RIGHT.

Small Wheel—left.   Large Wheel—right.

CHANGE—by sweeping both clubs in front and bringing them up on the right side, and halting them in position of point right. Make a small outward with the right hand, and a full sweep with the left, both clubs falling simultaneously.

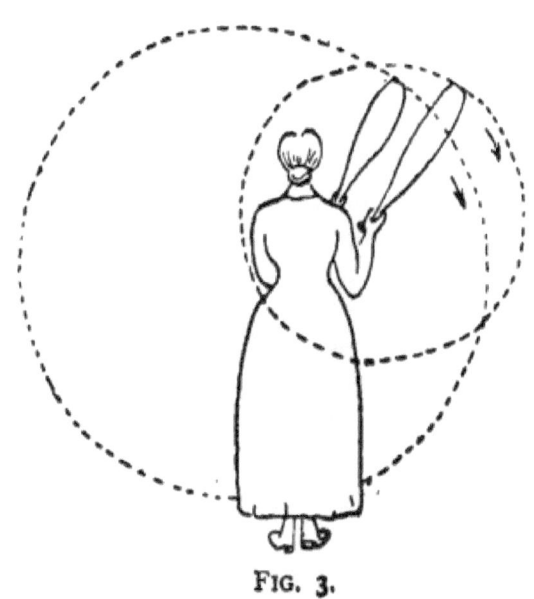

FIG. 3.

SMALL RIGHT.   LARGE LEFT.

Small Wheel—right.   Large Wheel—left.
   "   "   "   "   "   "
   "   "   "   "   "   "

CHANGE—by sweeping the clubs back to the left side and halting them a second, making a small outward with the left and a full sweep with the right. Sweep them both to the right side and halt a second making a small outward with the right and a full sweep with the left; thus alternating the movement from side to side.

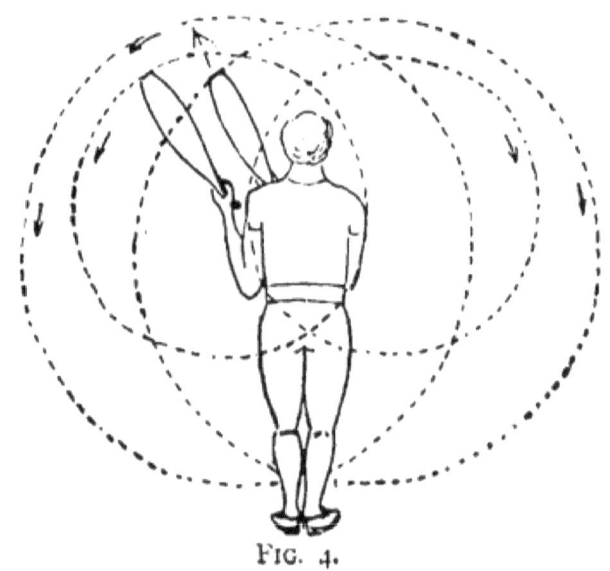

FIG. 4.

ALTERNATE.

Small left—Large right—Sweep. Small right—Large left—Sweep
  "   "   "   "   "   "   "   "
  "   "   "   "   "   "   "   "

CHANGE—by sweeping the clubs back to the left side and halting the club in the left hand at poise 1; but pass the right club up in front of the face and push it back of the head, letting it drop as if to make an inward. Instead of making a small circle, push it to the right, as shown in the illustration. As the right club drops behind the head, the left club sweeps back in front toward the right side. The clubs now change position—the left club is pushed back of the head, and the right club sweeps back in front.

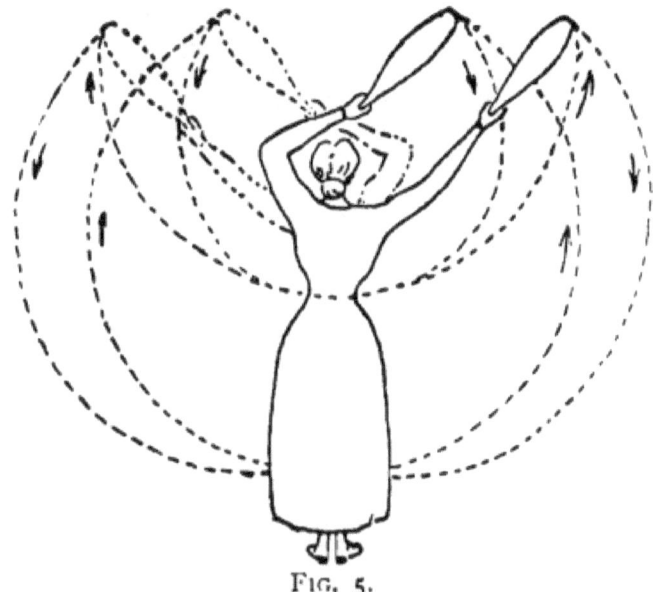

Fig. 5.

BACKWARD DROP.

Backward drop—right—push.   Backward drop—left—push.
    "   "   "   "   "   "   "   "
    "   "   "   "   "   "   "   "

CHANGE—by halting the left club at poise 1; swing it to poise 2; and drop it in front of the face. While this is being done the right club sweeps back on the circle in front, and halts at poise 1 on the right side, then to poise 2, and drops in front of the face; thus making the regular poise and drop with each hand.

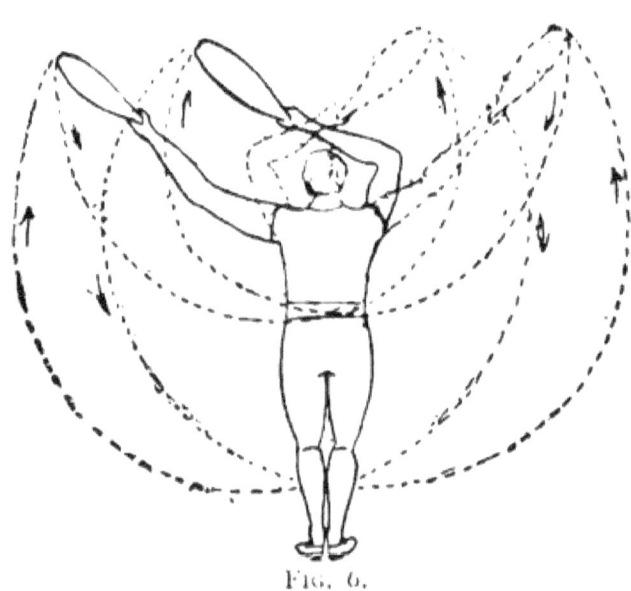

Fig. 6.

FORWARD DROP.

Poise and drop—Left.   Poise and drop—Right.

CHANGE.—by halting the clubs a second when they are on the left side. Turn the left club to an outward, while the right club passes down in front and sweeps up on the right side, making a small inward and push —as in the backward drop. It then sweeps down in front and is pushed back of the head, making a backward drop and push, while the left club is making an outward.

Fig. 7.

OUTWARD LEFT—BACKWARD DROP.

Outward left—Sweep.   Backward drop and push—Right.
"   "   "   "   "   "   "
"   "   "   "   "   "   "

CHANGE—by converting the backward push and drop of the right club, to an outward and sweep. When the club is pushed *right* the third time, instead of dropping it in front, turn it immediately to an outward. The left club makes no change but continues making the outward and sweep.

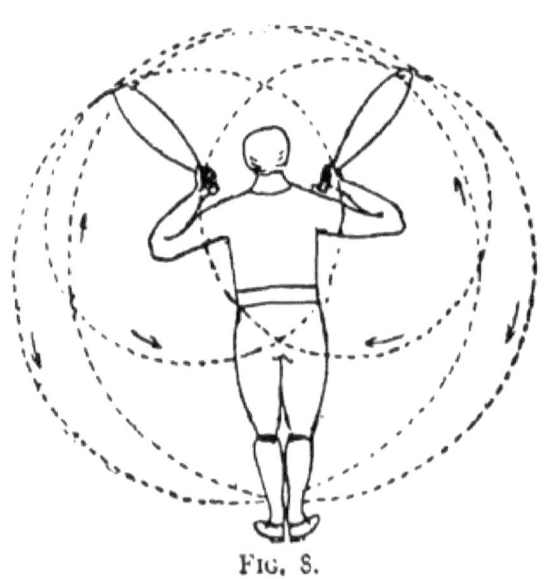

Fig. S.

ALTERNATING OUTWARD.

Outward left—Sweep.   Outward right—Sweep.

164   PHYSICAL TRAINING.

CHANGE—by halting both clubs a second, just as the *right* club closes the third small outward. Reverse it to a small inward, followed by a full sweep. The left club also reverses its movement, making a sweep, followed by a small inward. One club is making an inward while the other is making a sweep.

FIG. 9.

ALTERNATING INWARD.

Inward right—Sweep.   Inward left—Sweep.
   "   "   "   "   "   "
       "   "   "   Both clubs left side.

PHYSICAL TRAINING.   165

CHANGE—by making a small outward left, and a full sweep with the right; *i. e.*, what is known as small left, large right. Sweep both clubs in front at the same time, and bring them up on the right side, and sweep them up, over and back of the head, making small circles, both clubs parallel, as shown in the illustration.

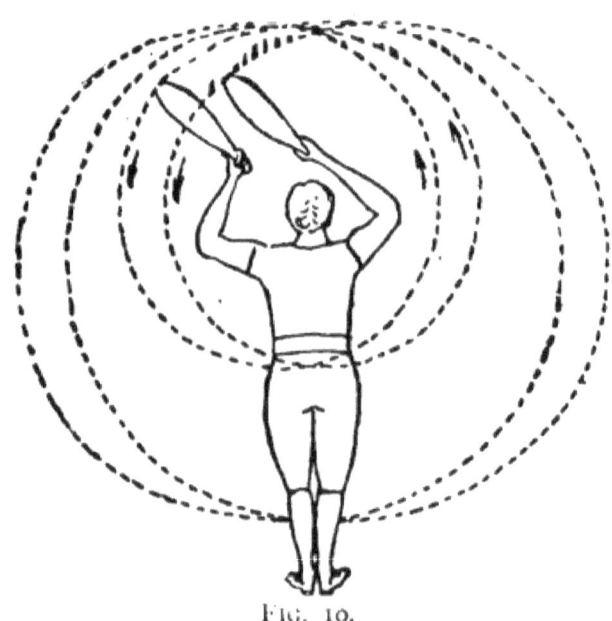

FIG. 10.

SMALL CIRCLES—BACK.

One small circle—Sweep
Two "   circles   "
Three "   "   Change.

166 PHYSICAL TRAINING.

CHANGE—by making an *extra* small circle with the left hand while the right sweeps in front. The right hand passes back to a small inward, while the left hand sweeps in front. By the time the small inward is finished with the right hand, the left will be in place for a small outward. The clubs now join, and make another double circle back of the head.

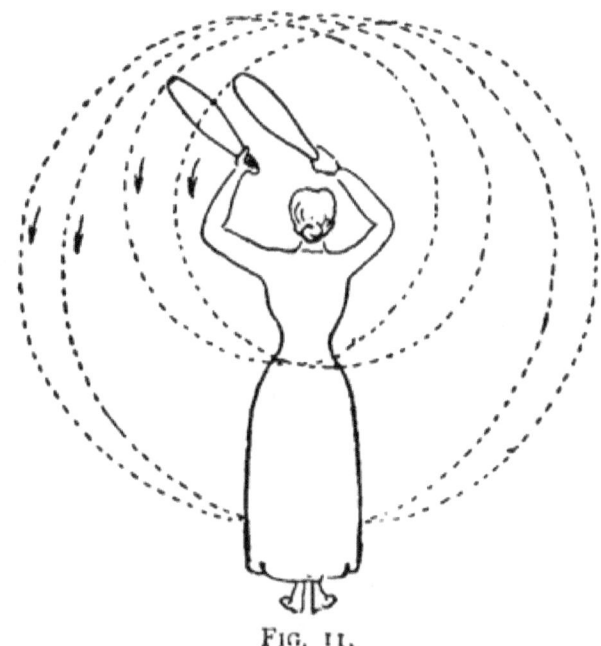

FIG. 11.

LEFT—RIGHT—BOTH.

Small left—Sweep.	Small right—Sweep.	Small—Both.
" " "	" " "	2 " "
" " "	" " "	3 " "

CHANGE—by pushing the left club up and out from the shoulder, while hastening the right in front, and making a full sweep, till—without halting either club—the right club is exactly opposite the left, just as the right passes the feet—both arms extended. The clubs should now follow each other, but neither *catch* the other. The right hand makes an inward and sweep, while the left is following with a sweep and outward.

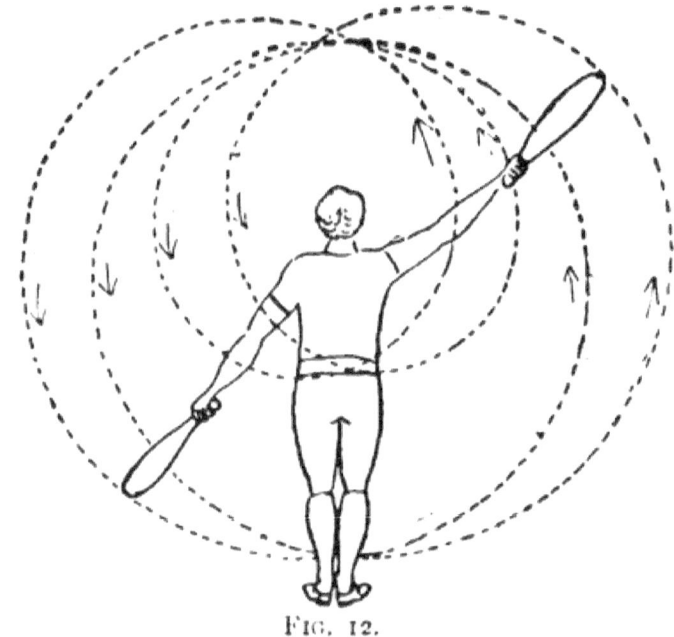

FIG. 12.

THE WINDMILL.

Inward right—Outward left—Sweep—Sweep.
    "   "   "   "   "   "
    "   "   "   "   omit sweep.

CHANGE—by slowing up on the left till the right now catches it. Sweep both clubs in front and back of the head (Fig. 10). Continue the small inward circles with the right hand, but shift the position of the left a trifle forward, making small side-circles. Both clubs should fall and rise at the same time, each crossing the track of the other. Swing them so that the circles are at right angles.

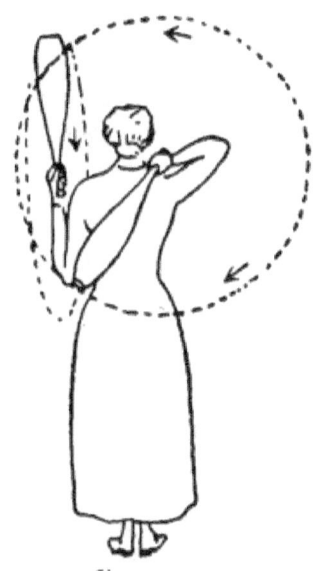

Fig. 13.

SIDE AND INWARD—LEFT.

Small side—Left.   Small inward—Right
"   "   "   "   "   "
"   "   "   "   "   "

CHANGE—by quickly shifting the clubs to the *right* side, making a small inward with the left, and a small side with the right.

FIG. 14.

SIDE AND INWARD—RIGHT.

Small side—Right.   Small inward—Left.
"   "   "   "   "   "
"   "   "   "   "   "

CHANGE—by shifting the clubs back to the left side, and then back to the right, continuing the same movement, but alternating from side to side.

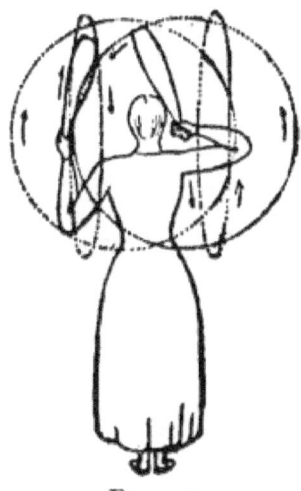

FIG. 15.

ALTERNATE.

Side and inward—Left.   Side and inward—Right.
"   "   "   "   "   "   "   "
"   "   "   "   "   "   "   "

CHANGE.—by bringing the clubs to a perpendicular poise on either side of the head. Make a small inward with the right, then a small inward with the left; again with the right, and again with the left. Sweep the right in front of the face, then the left, and bring them up to repeat the small inwards with each.

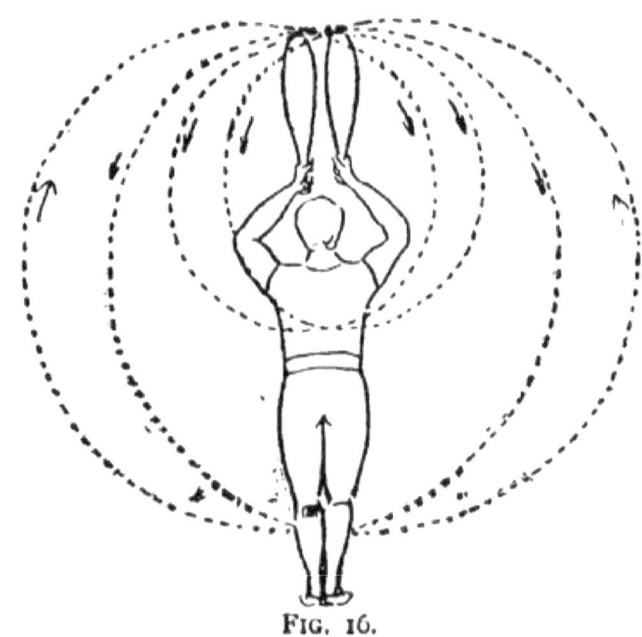

FIG. 16.

RIGHT—LEFT—RIGHT—LEFT—SWEEP—SWEEP.

Inward right- Inward left- Inward right- Inward left- Sweep-sweep.
    "   "   "   "   "   "   "   "   "
    "   "   "   "   "   "   "   omit sweep.

CHANGE.—by omitting the sweep the third time. At the conclusion of the small circles, bring the clubs again to a perpendicular poise on either side of the head, and make small side-circles; both clubs falling and rising simultaneously.

FIG. 17.

SMALL SIDES.

Small side—Right.	Small side—Left.	Together.
" " "	" " "	"
" " "	" " "	"

CHANGE—by bringing the clubs again to a perpendicular poise on either side of the head. Make small inwards with each hand at the same time, the clubs crossing each other at the handles.

FIG. 18.

SMALL INWARDS.

Small inward—Right.   Small inward—Left.   Together.
  "   "   "   "   "
  "   "   "   "   "

174 PHYSICAL TRAINING.

CHANGE—by sweeping both clubs in front of the face at the same time, crossing each other above and below in the circle. Keep the arms as fully extended as possible.

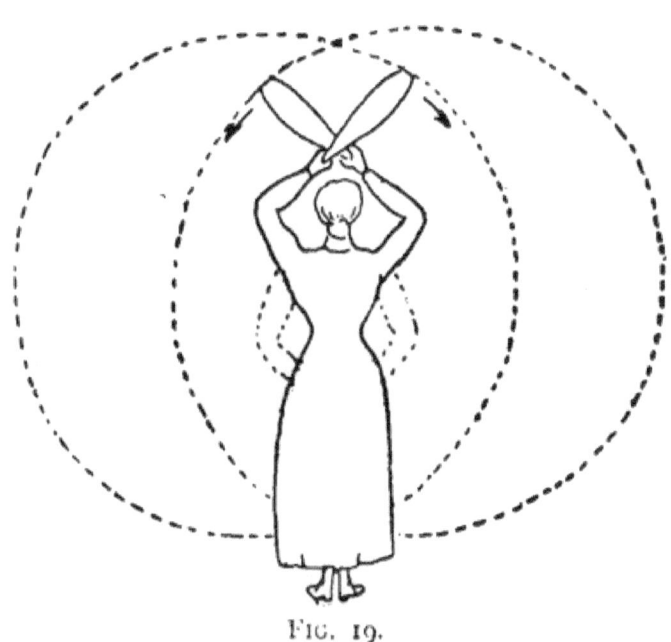

FIG. 19.

INWARD SWEEPS.

Sweep inward—Right.   Sweep inward—Left.   Together.

PHYSICAL TRAINING. 175

Change—by bringing the clubs again to a perpendicular poise on either side of the head, and then unite the last three moves in one; *i. e.*, giving them in succession—one of each.

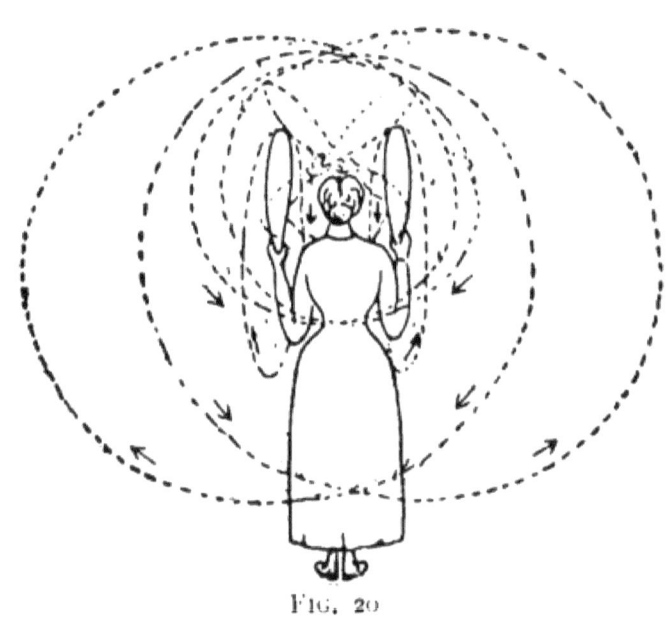

Fig. 20

SIDE—INWARD—SWEEP.

Small sides—Small inwards—Sweeps.
"   "   "   "   "
"   "   "   "   "
"   " change.

CHANGE—by bringing the clubs again to a perpendicular poise, and swing them to small circles toward the left (Fig. 10). Then turn the body quickly to the left—without moving the left foot. Make small side-circles once. Sweep the clubs together, bringing them up on the *right* side. Turn the body right—without moving the right foot, and make small side-circles once. Sweep the clubs back to the left side and repeat. Both clubs should fall together—only one club being visible to any one sitting directly opposite.

FIG. 21.

SMALL SIDE—LEFT AND RIGHT.

1 Small side—Left—Sweep.   1 Small side—Right—Sweep.
2   "   "   "   "   2   "   "   "   "
3   "   "   "   "   3   "   "   omit sweep.

CHANGE.—by halting the left club as it points up till the right club points down. Instead of the clubs falling simultaneously, they now fall successively.

Fig. 22.

ALTERNATE.

Small sides.	Down—Right.	Down—Left.
,, ,,	,, ,,	,, ,,
,, ,,	,, ,,	,, ,,

178   PHYSICAL TRAINING.

CHANGE—by halting the right club when it points up, till the left club also points up. Continue the small side-circle forward, with the *left* hand, but reverse the small side-circle with the *right* hand. Again both clubs fall simultaneously, though in opposite directions.

FIG. 23.

REVERSE.

Small sides.   Forward—Left.   Reverse—Right
   "   "   "   "
   "   "   "   "

CHANGE—by making small sides and sweeping to the left side. Turn the body to the left, without moving the left foot. Make small sides as soon as the clubs come up on the left side; then make small circles again, but pass both clubs *inside* the arms; then again small sides *outside;* then thrust both clubs under the arms, as shown in the illustration. Then toss the clubs up for small sides again.

FIG. 24.

DOUBLE CHIN-KNOCKER.

Small circles—Outside—Inside—Outside—Under. Toss.
    "   "   "   "   "
    "   "   "   "   "
                            "   sweep.

CHANGE—by sweeping the clubs in front—now facing front. Check the right club when the arm and club are perfectly horizontal. Push the left club back of the head and make a small inward—left three times, while holding the right hand and club perfectly quiet. Sweep the left club in front, make a poise and drop, and, *as* it drops, sweep the right club down with it.

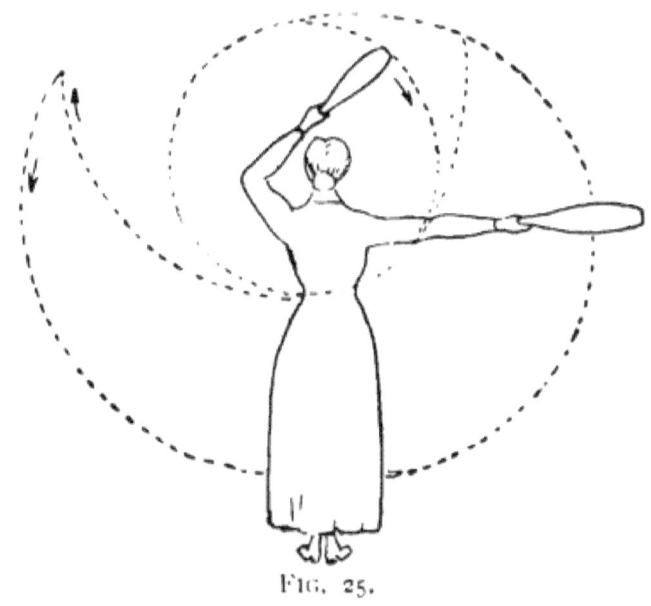

FIG. 25.

RIGHT HORIZONTAL.

Horizontal—Right. Inward 1—Left.
       " 2 "
       " 3 " and sweep.
   Poise and drop—Left. Sweep both.

CHANGE—by sweeping the clubs up to the left side, holding the *left* arm horizontal, and passing the *right* club back of the head. Make three small inward circles with the right hand, then sweep in front of the face, and make a poise and drop with the right hand.

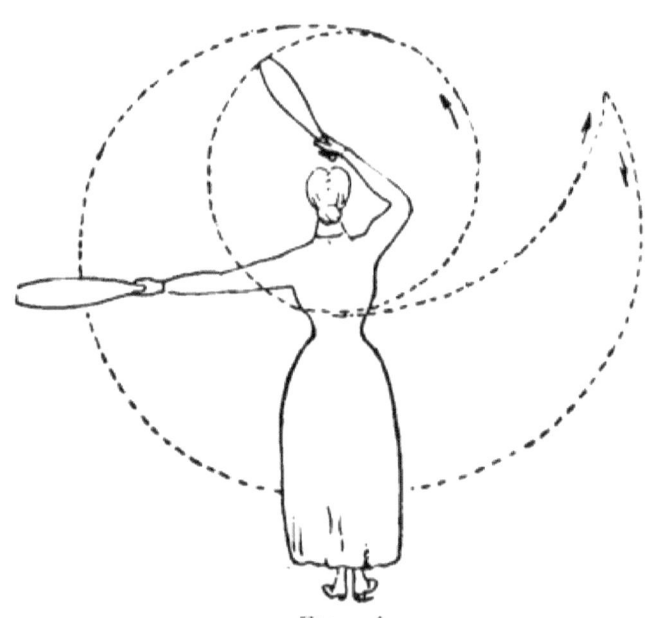

FIG. 26.

LEFT HORIZONTAL.

Horizontal—Left. Inward 1—Right.
     " 2 "
     " 3 " and sweep.
  Poise and drop—Right—Sweep both,

CHANGE—by sweeping the clubs to a small circle back of the head (Fig. 10). Turn the body squarely to the left—the weight on both feet. Make small sides simultaneously; then sweep them to the floor, and pass them as far back as possible without bending the arms or the body. Do not allow the clubs to wabble. Check the clubs quickly and pass them at once up and back of the head, and check them. Do not allow them to swing loosely toward the back. Swing again to small sides.

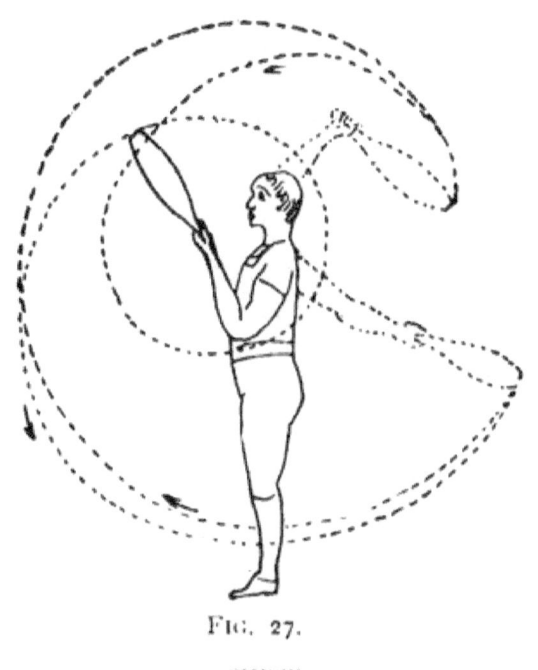

FIG. 27.

CHECK.

1 Small side—Sweep—Check.   Up—Check.
2   "   "   "   "   "
3   "   "   change.

CHANGE—by making an extra small side-circle with the left hand, while the right makes a large side-circle. Then make a small side-circle with the *right* hand, and a *large* side-circle with the left. Both clubs should fall with the same impulse—the one making a large circle, while the other makes a small.

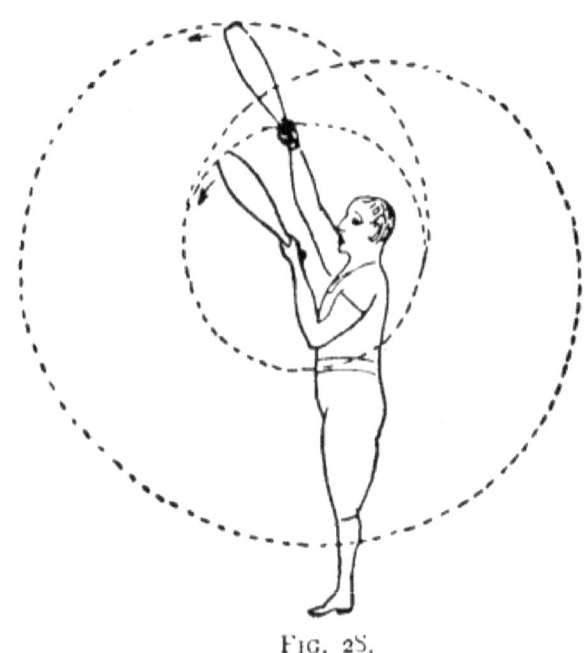

Fig. 28.

SHOULDER BRACE.

Small left—Large right.   Small right—Large left.
 "   "   "   "   "   "   "   "
 "   "   "   "   change.

CHANGE—by checking the large side-circle, with the right hand, just as the club has passed a short distance back of the feet. At the same time extend the left arm and club up and forward—pointing exactly opposite the right. Slip the right foot a little back of the left—the momentum of the club on the downward sweep will aid you. With a quick but strong impulse sweep both clubs at once in opposite directions—the left arm makes a large circle forward, the right arm a large side-circle reversed. Keep the arms unbent and close to the body.

FIG. 29.

LARGE REVERSE.

Large side—Forward—Left.   Large side—Backward—Right.

PHYSICAL TRAINING. 185

CHANGE—by halting the right club as it sweeps up in front on the third reverse. Let it fall to a small side. Check the left club as it passes the feet the third time, and bring it up in front with a sweep. It will reach there in time to join the right club as it makes a second small side-circle. Join them (both making a small side), sweep them to the front (turning the body front), and pass them back of the head, making small circles back (Fig. 10). Pass directly to the *windmill*, and add small side alternates (Fig. 22).

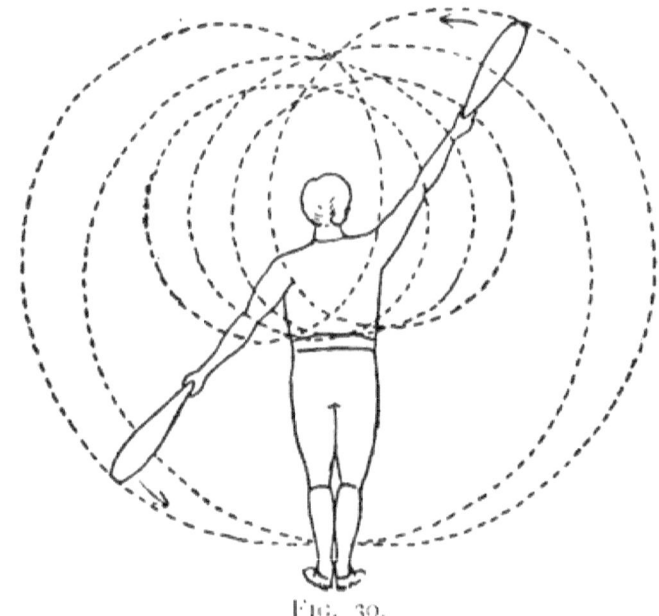

FIG. 30.

WINDMILL.—ALTERNATE.

Inward right—Outward left—Small side right—Small side left—Sweep. Sweep.
Inward right—Outward left—Small side right—Small side left—Sweep. Sweep.
Inward right—Outward left—Small side right—Small side left—Sweep both.

THE FINISH.

Halt the right club when completing the third small alternate, till the left club comes up on the third small circle. Sweep both in front with one impulse, and pass them back over the head to a small circle (Fig. 10.). Follow this with a small side-circle (Fig. 21). Pass the clubs gracefully under the arms (Fig. 24). Keep them there till you have made your bow and exit.

WARMAN'S INDIAN-CLUB SYSTEM.
TWO CLUBS.

TO TAKE THEM ARTISTICALLY FROM THE FLOOR.

Face front. Stand between the clubs. Fold the arms. With the first note of the music, unfold the arms, raise the hands above the head, and sweep them down to the side. Bend the body, take the clubs with sufficient impulse to sweep them a short distance back. Straighten the body, and this will give the clubs an impulse forward. Sweep them up high enough in front to make small side circles (Fig. 17), then small circles back of the head (Fig. 10), then, turning the body quickly to the left, make small side circles (Fig. 21), halting them in position of Fig. 1—two clubs.

N. B.—In *class* exhibitions we would advise the pupils to leave the platform at the close of the one-club exercise, and when they return, *carry* the two clubs under the arms, as shown in Fig. 24. At a signal from the music, toss the clubs in front to the same position as when sweeping them up from the floor.

We herewith present our system of exercises:

CONDENSED FOR CALLING—TWO CLUBS.

No. 1. Point Left. Right—Left.
　　　　　　　　　　　"　　　"
　　　　　　　　　　　"　　　"

No. 2. Small left—Large right. 1-2-3. Sweep.
No. 3. Small right—Large left. 1-2-3. Sweep.
No. 4. Alternate. Left—Right.
　　　　　　　　　　"　　　"
　　　　　　　　　　"　　　" sweep.

No. 5. Backward drop. Right—Left.
　　　　　　　　　　　　"　　　"
　　　　　　　　　　　　"　　　"

No. 6. Forward drop. Left—Right.
　　　　　　　　　　　"　　　"
　　　　　　　　　　　"　　　"

No. 7. Outward left—Backward drop, right.
　　　　　　"　　　　　　　　　　"
　　　　　　"　　　　　　　　　　"

No. 8. Alternating outward. Left—Right.
　　　　　　　　　　　　　　"　　　"
　　　　　　　　　　　　　　"　　　"

No. 9. Alternating inward. Right—Left.
　　　　　　　　　　　　　"　　　"
　　　　　　　　　　　　　　" sweep.

No. 10. Small back-circles. 1—Sweep.
　　　　　　　　　　　　　 2　 "
　　　　　　　　　　　　　 3 change.

No. 11. Left—Right—Both 1
　　　　　"　　　"　　　"　 2
　　　　　"　　　"　　　"　 3 change.

No. 12. Windmill. 1-2-3.
No. 13. Side and inward—Left side. 1-2-3.
No. 14. Side and inward—Right side. 1-2-3.
No. 15. Alternate. Left—Right.
       " "
       " "

No. 16. Right—Left— Right—Left —Sweep—Sweep.
    " " " " " "
    " " " " Halt.

No. 17. Small sides. 1-2-3.
No. 18. Small inwards. 1-2-3.
No. 19. Double sweep. 1-2-3.
No. 20. Small side—Inward—Sweep.
     " " "
     " " "
     " Turn.

No. 21. Small sides, left-one. Small sides, right-one.
    " " " two " " " two.
    " " " three " " " three.

No. 22. Alternate. Right—Left.
       " "
       '

No. 23. Reverse 1-2-3. Sweep to left side.
No. 24. Out—In—Out—Under. Toss.
    " " " " "
    " " " " "
    " and sweep.

No. 25. Right—Horizontal.
   Left—Inward. 1-2-3. Sweep.
    " Poise and drop.
     Take it along (the right).

No. 26. Left—Horizontal.
       Right—Inward. 1-2-3. Sweep.
          " Poise and drop.
            Take it along (the left). Sweep—turn

No. 27. Small sides and check. Up.
      " " two " "
      " " three

No. 28. Shoulder brace. Left—Right.
           " "
           " reverse.

No. 29. Large reverse. 1-2-3.

No. 30. Windmill and alternate. 1-2-3.

Sweep the clubs under the arms, and make your exit.

BOXING GLOVES.

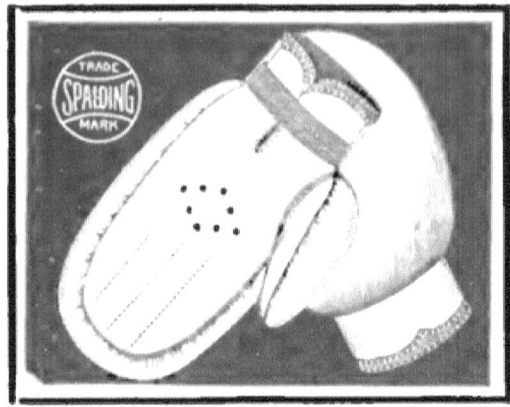

We would call special attention to those interested in the manly art of self-defence, to our superior line of Boxing gloves. We have arranged in our new factory a special room for manufacturing these goods, and will make an extra quality of gloves, out of the very best material, and on the latest improved patterns. Manufacturing as we do, in very large quantities, we are enabled to offer our customers these superior gloves at comparatively low prices, and can recommend them as superior to any other glove on the market.

Each glove from 40 up, will bear our trade-mark to insure its genuineness, and will be known as "Spalding's Trade marked Boxing Gloves."

PRICE LIST.

		Per Set of Four Gloves
No. AA.	Boys' size, same as No. BB....	$1 50
No. BB.	Men's size Boxing Gloves, chamois back, tan palms; cheapest glove made..................	2 00
No. A.	Boys' size, same as No. B	2 50
No. B.	Men's size Boxing Gloves, chamois back with tan palm; new style; strong and durable ...	3 00
No. C.	White Kid, tan palms; same style as No. D.........	4 00
No. D.	All White Kid, made after the new pattern.	4 50
No. 30.	Glove is made with chamois back, tan palm; strong and well made	3 50
No. 40.	An all Buckskin Glove, made of fine quality buck; very soft, large, and nice for amateurs	5 00
No. 45.	Same as No. 40, heel padded	5 50
No. 50.	A superior Glove, kid back, tan palm; the most durable and best glove made at the price	5 50
No. 55.	A superior Glove, well made, kid back, buckskin palm.....	6 00
No. 60.	Fine White Kid, large size, fully stuffed; a soft, light glove for amateurs; ventilated palm	6 50
No. 65.	Same as No. 60; heel padded	7 00
No. 70.	Professional (or Chandler's) White Kid Glove; same style as used by Chandler, Sullivan, and other well known boxers; a perfect glove for expert boxers	7 00
No. 75.	Four-ounce Professional Exhibition Fighting Glove, used by well known boxers for severe slugging	6 00
No. 75A	Two-ounce Hard Fighting Glove	6 00
No. 80.	Graham's Patent Safety Glove; made of finest material, with Graham's patent safety tip	7 00
No. 85.	Same as No. 80; heel padded	7 50

CHICAGO. A. G. SPALDING & BROS. NEW YORK.
PHILADELPHIA. LONDON.

INDIAN CLUBS.

In introducing our new Trade-marked Indian Clubs, we would call special attention to the perfect shape, beautiful ebony finish, and correct weight of each club. We select the very choicest timber for these clubs, turn them by hand, and work each club down to the exact troy weight, and this care in making, together with the beautiful ebony finish, highly polished, and banded in gold, with nickel-plated heads, makes them the most beautiful and desirable Indian Clubs ever placed upon the market. We purpose keeping these clubs up to the very highest grade, and to protect ourselves and customers against cheap imitations, our trade-mark will be stamped on each club, as represented in the above cut. The following very low prices will make these clubs very popular.

Prices of Spalding's Trade-marked Indian Clubs.

Weight		Price
1 lb.	per pair,	$1 00
2 lbs.	"	1 10
3 lbs.	"	1 35
4 lbs.	"	1 70
5 lbs.	"	2 00
6 lbs.	"	2 25

CHICAGO. A. G. SPALDING & BROS. NEW YORK.
PHILADELPHIA. LONDON.

www.ingramcontent.com/pod-product-compliance
Lightning Source LLC
Chambersburg PA
CBHW032143160426
43197CB00008B/765